MANAGING
ELECTRONIC
RESERVES

JEFF ROSEDALE
Editor

**AMERICAN
LIBRARY
ASSOCIATION**
Chicago and
London
2002

Cover design by Tracey Harris

Text design by Dianne M. Rooney

Composition by ALA Editions in Sabon and Avant Garde using QuarkXpress on a PC platform

Printed on 50-pound white offset, a pH-neutral stock, and bound in 10-point cover stock by McNaughton & Gunn

While extensive effort has gone into ensuring the reliability of information appearing in this book, the publisher makes no warranty, express or implied, on the accuracy or reliability of the information, and does not assume and hereby disclaims any liability to any person for any loss or damage caused by errors or omissions in this publication.

The paper used in this publication meets the minimum requirements of American National Standard for Information Sciences—Permanence of Paper for Printed Library Materials, ANSI Z39.48-1992. ⊚

ISBN 0-8389-0812-8

Printed in the United States of America

06 05 04 03 02   5 4 3 2 1

CONTENTS

iv　　　　　　　　　　　　　　　*Contents*

PREFACE

Talking to people about electronic reserves can elicit some interesting reactions. Some still seem to think that this is a less-than-legitimate area of academic librarianship. A caricature may be used to illustrate this:

> A publishing executive turns in the night, her sleep disturbed by a vivid nightmare: Deep inside the halls of a venerable college campus, a renegade group of access-crazy techie librarians are scanning the entire contents of hundreds of textbooks, cover to cover, with wild abandon and mounting them on a web page with no restrictions. They are doing this just because the technology exists to do so, and without any thoughts about the repercussions of their actions. They excitedly talk of their status as pioneers of a twenty-first century economics, where information is "free for all."
>
> In the background, a crackling fire consumes the text of U.S.C. title 17, the Copyright Act, along with a pile of dollar bills representing the publisher's lost revenue stream. The digitized contents of the textbooks are electronically transmitted to trillions of eager consumers who repackage, alter, and resell them within minutes.
>
> Sometimes the dream ends with the publisher sitting on a cold street corner, broke and discredited. An alternative ending features the librarians being hauled away by the National Guard, with Old Glory waving and reaffirming the sure victory of truth, justice, and the American way.

In order to examine the realities of electronic reserves, it is necessary to understand the meaning of the term and why it is an important element in the bundle of services academic and research libraries can provide. Without excessive reproduction of the chapters that follow, here is a distillation of these underpinnings: Electronic reserves involves some combination of creating, storing, organizing, providing access to, and managing digital objects representing items that faculty have selected to be used directly in conjunction with their instructional activities.

Reformatting materials is often part of electronic reserves. The service may also depend on receipt and organization of objects already existing in digital form. Items may fall entirely within the public domain, may be commercially published, or may be the sole property of individual authors (often the teaching faculty themselves). Policies regarding user access, length of time that materials are stored, and management of copyright permissions vary by institution. Electronic reserve collections and services, like their traditional counterparts, are highly individual!

The difficulty in narrowing down a definition of electronic reserves and the lack of any single methodology that carries the equivalent of a Good Housekeeping Seal of Approval are intrinsic to the nature of reserve services in general. Since faculty play the key role in defining the nature and scope of course reserve materials, it is virtually impossible to generalize efforts to predict, administer, or quantify the needs and demands associated with their delivery.

Reserve services can be vexing to all parties connected with them: the faculty member who wants an article made available to his class tomorrow; the student who finds the library closed at 11:05 the night before an exam; the staff member who has to order or reproduce another copy of an item that was stolen or damaged by overuse; the library administrator who has to find a way to reduce the long lines at the reserve desk.

Libraries and librarians have pursued electronic reserves because it is a fast, convenient, flexible, and powerful way to meet the informational needs of students and faculty. Increasingly, the degree to which technology is applied to facilitate the learning experience on college and university campuses is an indicator of competitiveness. How "wired" a campus is may play a role in a student's decision to attend a school or an alumnus's decision to support it with donations. Libraries have responded to an environment filled with self-service kiosks; students and faculty who expect the world to be delivered to real, virtual, and mobile desktops; and 24/7 service demands.

The development of electronic reserves is largely a grassroots phenomenon. From the early experiments at San Diego State University with reserve readings on a local area network through the advent of the open source software movement, many of the movers and shakers in electronic reserves have been ordinary professors and academic librarians. They simply sought to improve a vital element of instructional support by harnessing the power of technology. State and private, small and large, college and university—all eventually discovered a common interest in electronic reserves.

Fortunately, even in an environment treating virtually all forms of information as a commodity, these pioneers were not dissuaded from experimentation. From the earliest implementation of electronic reserves, the idea of balancing rights and responsibilities in handling intellectual property was woven into the design and delivery of services. Much thought has been devoted to the merits of delivering text versus image files, determining means of authentication and authorization, soliciting copyright permissions, and staking out a place for fair use in the digital realm.

It is less clear how much users' needs have been factored into the design and delivery of electronic reserve services. This is due in part to the insular nature of the traditional and e-reserves communities. Ever since the *Kinko's* case in the early 1980s, libraries have run their reserves with some degree of paranoia. In the mid-1990s, the Association of American Publishers was rumored to be creating a war chest specifically for lawsuits against copyright violators, among which libraries were perceived to be prominent. As a result of these trends, libraries went about designing improvements to their reserves without a great deal of public discussion and a notable lack of research.

Administrative ambivalence toward reserve services still exists in many forms. The staffing cuts of the 1980s and 1990s forced administrators to look for places to cut, and the sizable reserves units made easy targets. Libraries, it was argued, simply couldn't afford to provide the bundle of services that faculty had become accustomed to. As a result, many libraries offload the responsibility of copyright compliance onto faculty, washing their hands of this part of the service. The practice of making or obtaining copies of articles became particularly burdensome. In these circumstances, some wished that reserve collections would be made obsolete by the widespread use of coursepacks or that outsourcing would reduce or even eliminate library reserve services.

Any reserve service is expensive and complicated to design, manage, and maintain, regardless of format. Faculty selection—often at the last minute—makes it difficult to predict the type and amount of material in a reserve collection. The variety of formats, publishers, time periods, countries of origin, and sheer bulk of material represented from one reserve collection to another is staggering. Sciences collections may be rich in graphic images and high in faculty-produced materials (tests, lecture notes, etc.). Humanities collections may contain numerous editions of the same works, including some older editions that have passed into the public domain. Music and art collections are full of multimedia items.

Going electronic does not make these complexities go away, but it can provide an opportunity to reestablish guidelines that prioritize effective and consistent service. More importantly, it represents a unique opportunity to cement relationships among faculty, students, librarians, and technical staff. These relationships will certainly be a key to libraries' remaining relevant in a future characterized by accelerating change.

In a 1998 panel presentation at a meeting of the American Society for Information Science, I formulated a slightly radical notion. The title of the presentation referred to a "clash of stakeholders on the information superhighway." I thought about that and decided that "shareholders" might be a more useful term. To my mind, a stakeholder is banking on defending and leveraging a fixed position; shareholders can debate and disagree, but their success depends on defining and building areas of common interest—something strong and solid enough to be lasting, but flexible enough to cope with change. A shareholder is cognizant of the ways in which different parts of a process feed one another in order to support the growth and development of larger processes.

In order to build intellectual capital, which is the lifeblood of educators, publishers, and libraries alike, a dispassionate analysis of combining strengths and serving needs is required. I hope this book will spur more of this kind of work. I also hope it encourages investment in the people, facilities, and technologies it takes to get the most out of course reserve services and to build what lies beyond.

ACKNOWLEDGMENTS

The following individuals and organizations have been critically important in the development of electronic reserves in general, and this book in particular. All deserve heartfelt thanks.

The Association of Research Libraries: Duane Webster and Mary Jackson have been supporting member and nonmember institutions in their efforts to provide electronic reserve services since 1994. Through sponsorship of the arl-ereserve discussion list and workshops that have educated people from hundreds of institutions, ARL has done more than any single organization to promote awareness and understanding of electronic reserves.

The copyright experts: Laura Gasaway and Kenneth Crews have helped explore the intellectual property issues in developing this new digital library service. It takes special talent to explain copyright issues comprehensively but in terms that anyone can understand. Understanding how to deal with intellectual property in electronic reserve systems has been a key component in fostering their growth and acceptance.

The ACRL electronic reserves discussion group, meeting at ALA Annual and Midwinter conferences, continues to provide a forum for practitioners to showcase their systems and discuss successes, failures, needs, and challenges—reminding us that there is still no acceptable substitute for face-to-face interaction.

The pioneers: Don Bosseau, Brian Nielsen, Phil Kesten, and the many others who shaped the building blocks from which modern e-reserve systems and policies have been crafted.

The contributors to and publisher of this book, who made the ideas come to life.

My inspiration: my wife, Mary, whose support and encouragement make all things possible.

1

Frequently Asked Questions about Electronic Reserves

LORRE SMITH

1. General Electronic Reserves Information and Resources

Q. 1.1   What is electronic reserves?
Q. 1.1.1   Is electronic reserves a type of "courseware"?
Q. 1.2   Why should our library offer electronic reserves?
Q. 1.3   Where can I get more information about electronic reserves?
Q. 1.4   Is there an association involved in electronic reserves?
Q. 1.5   Which institutions are offering electronic reserves?
Q. 1.6   If I implement electronic reserves can I close the reserves desk?
Q. 1.7   Can electronic reserves be outsourced?

2. Equipment

Q. 2.1   What equipment do I need for electronic reserves?
Q. 2.1.1   Can I buy a turnkey system?
Q. 2.1.2   What happens if the system goes down?
Q. 2.2   What equipment should I have for scanning text?
Q. 2.3   What equipment should I have to manage audiovisual files?
Q. 2.4   How should I choose a web server?

3. Software

4. Operations Policies and Procedures

5. Staffing

1. GENERAL INFORMATION AND RESOURCES

1.1 What is electronic reserves?

Electronic reserves derives its name from the print reserve services offered by academic libraries. The print services go by several other names, including short loan and course reserves, but electronic reserves is the name most frequently used by librarians who wish to offer the information previously loaned out from the reserve service unit (or whatever it has been called).

John Kupersmith (jkup@jkup.net), a consultant to the Association of Research Libraries, defined the following types of reserve services:

TRADITIONAL RESERVES. In a designated area of the library, required or recommended readings for courses are placed on reserve by faculty request and made available to students, usually with short loan periods or other restrictions to ensure that everyone needing an item has some access to it. Students generally learn about these items through reserve lists provided by faculty. Reserve materials may be in any format, including books, photocopies of chapters or journal articles, notes or problem sets provided by faculty, audiovisual items, etc. The library may also place on reserve other types of material (such as archival collections of dissertations or yearbooks) that are vulnerable to theft or deterioration. There is generally no charge for access to reserve materials, but many students use coin- or card-operated photocopiers to make copies for later use.

AUTOMATED RESERVES. Reserve materials are listed in the library's online catalog or other database system so students can look them up by instructor's name, course number, etc. An automated circulation system is used to check out, check in, and track the status of reserve items. Physical access to, and use of, the material is the same as with traditional reserve services.

ELECTRONIC RESERVES. The actual reserve materials are stored in electronic format—typically ASCII text or graphic images—for access, retrieval, viewing, downloading, or printing by students. Depending on the system design, this access may take place through remote network and dial-up connections as well as in the library. Users may be required to pay a fee, such as a per-page charge when printing or downloading.[1]

1.1.1 Is electronic reserves a type of "courseware"?

Courseware may include some of the functions currently performed by electronic reserve systems. Courseware also includes course management functions such as online quizzes, record keeping for grades and other files, and interactive features that go beyond the storage and retrieval of readings or other course materials such as videos or audio recordings.

1.2 Why should our library offer electronic reserves?

Traditional problems of print reserves involved the short circulation period, the high fines for overdue materials, high loss and mutilation rate, and the inaccessibility of materials when the library is closed during traditional high-use periods such as midterm and final exams. Electronic reserves offers access to course readings via an electronic network, which means that circulation from the library and the consequent issues are no longer relevant. Students are not restricted by library hours of operation or limited loan periods. Readings cannot be mutilated or stolen, so they are available to all as part of the course materials on the electronic reserve system. Reproduction is often of a high quality. The advantages are substantial. If the network infrastructure is in place, electronic reserve services can become as routine as print reserve services, with few of the disadvantages.

1.3 Where can I get more information about electronic reserves?

At the time of this writing, there is not a general print source beyond the book you are reading now, but there is a growing body of articles that may be retrieved through bibliographic databases concerning library science. Three substantial sources for general and specific information are on the World Wide Web.

- The Association of Research Libraries-ereserve forum (arl-ereserve) archives hold the collective wisdom of electronic reserve providers. Information can be retrieved by simple keyword search, date, author, and subject thread. For access to the archives, go to www.cni.org/Hforums/arl-ereserve/. The arl-ereserve is an ongoing electronic discussion of electronic reserve issues. To subscribe and find out more about the forum, go to the web site and follow the subscription instructions: www.cni.org/Hforums/arl-ereserve/about.html. Members of the forum include providers of electronic reserve services. Contributors range from novices to highly experienced practitioners.

- Jeff Rosedale's Electronic Reserves Clearinghouse: Links and Materials on the Web (www.mville.edu/Administration/staff/Jeff_Rosedale) contains a wide variety of links to information about all aspects of electronic reserves. A list of approximately 150 international links to current electronic reserve systems allows you to see what other libraries and organizations have up and running.

1.4 Is there an association involved in electronic reserves?

The American Library Association (ALA), Association of College and Research Libraries (ACRL) electronic reserves discussion group meets regularly at the Annual and Midwinter conferences; consult the ALA web pages (www.ala.org) for conference schedules.

1.5 Who is offering electronic reserves?

All sizes of libraries are offering electronic reserves. Some systems are created in-house with existing resources, and some are purchased from vendors. The Electronic Reserves Clearinghouse: Links and Materials on the Web (www.mville.edu/Administration/staff/Jeff_ Rosedale) provides links to many current systems. The links are organized by the name of the institution, so they give an excellent overview of which schools and organizations are currently offering the services.

1.6 If I implement electronic reserves can I close the reserve desk?

Don't get your hopes up. Judging from discussions in the arl-ereserve forum and in the ACRL discussion group, many libraries still have a print reserve operation of some kind. Some libraries no longer circulate photocopies from the reserve desk and retain only a small number of materials. They circulate only what they cannot (or will not) reformat. This includes full books and other resources that may present significant problems in electronic format. For the most up-to-date information, consult arl-ereserve, the electronic discussion described above.

1.7 Can electronic reserves be outsourced?

Xerox Digital Curriculum Online Reserves, explained on the Xerox web site, seems to be claiming the spot as an outsource for electronic reserve services, and it seems to be the only possibility as of this writing. The web site gives contact information for representatives.

2. EQUIPMENT

2.1 What equipment do I need for electronic reserves?

In general, electronic reserves requires a scanner and a workstation to manage the scanning process and the scanned files. Each library staff must decide how many workstations to assign to electronic reserves. A file server that allows access to the files is needed for distribution to library users. All the equipment required to connect the workstations and the server to the campus infrastructure must be in place as well.

Scanning

The scanner is required if electronic reserve services include the reformatting of print resources into electronic files. The workstation is usually connected to the network that will provide the files to the end users so that the files can be uploaded to the network and maintained from the workstation once they are scanned. Many librarians have reported that they need a document feed to handle the quantity of pages they need to process at busy times in the semester.

Maintaining reserve files

More staff workstations may be required to access the files, depending upon the locations of the staff members who will be working with them. These workstations should all be connected to the network that includes the file server equipment.

Serving the files on a network

The files are almost always stored on a server that is available 24 hours a day, commonly a web server. A backup server will ensure service in times of highest volume. Instead of purchasing individual servers for electronic reserves, some libraries use existing servers in the library or in another institutional unit. Users of electronic reserves will require equipment capable of retrieving, displaying, and printing.

A systems analysis and design student project paper from Indiana University has described a system for electronic reserves. It's in the archives of the arl-ereserve forum (www.cni.org/Hforums/arl-ereserve/) in a post with the subject "Graham Shepfer <gshepfer@memex.lib.indiana. edu>: IU Reserves" by Jeff Rosedale, dated Feb. 21, 1994.

2.1.1 Can I buy a complete system that is designed and configured for electronic reserves?

Yes, you can. Several electronic reserve providers have also created systems with in-house resources. There are many vendors and products at this writing, and the Electronic Reserves Clearinghouse page (www. mville.edu/Administration/staff/Jeff_Rosedale) is likely to have the most current list.

2.1.2 What happens if the system goes down?

That's a question different providers answer in different ways. Since libraries handle computing resources in a wide variety of ways, it is not possible to give one single answer. Many libraries provide backup equipment that holds all of the electronic reserve systems and files, and it may be substituted for the system that goes down. It may be less cumbersome to provide manual backups. Each library staff must assess the cost/benefit ratio of providing different types of backup for their users.

2.2 What equipment should I have for scanning text or images?

Scanners come in a variety of sizes. There are flatbed, overhead, and drum scanners that can handle different materials and volume levels at varying levels of speed. Scanning software requirements should be taken into account when scanners are considered for purchase. Electronic reserves will require reformatting of a variety of materials, but most will be photocopies of 8½ × 11-inch sheets of paper.

As with all equipment, the library staff must determine what materials will be accepted for electronic reserves and must make intelligent estimates of the volume at peak periods. It is probably wise to select a scanner that can handle estimated maximums plus more to take into account that it may be an astonishingly popular service. Scanners and their controlling software offer a good array of options for control of the quality of the scanned file. Users of reserve readings may wish to handle files in many ways as well as read them from the screen, so select scanners that will provide the best possible image.

Scanning equipment is a frequent topic of the arl-ereserve discussion group. Colleagues can provide up-to-date information and equipment selection tips.

2.3 What equipment should I have for audiovisual files?

Audiovisual files are not served as frequently as text and image files in electronic reserves. Digital recording capability is the most important aspect. Just as with text and image files, electronic reserve users want the best quality in the most easily transmitted file. Sound files are usually music recordings or foreign language study materials, so sound quality is very important. Video files can vary greatly, from art productions to documentaries. Reserve staff must balance sound and visual quality with reasonable file size.

Once the files are produced, an audiovisual file server should be acquired for distribution. Take into consideration all the equipment features necessary to connect the server to the existing delivery infrastructure.

2.4 How should I choose a web server?

System vendors will probably offer recommendations for appropriate equipment and help you get in touch with their current customers so you can ask questions and make comparisons. Some systems provide all the necessary equipment, and some offer the system software for purchase, to be installed on library equipment. Investigate different electronic reserve products to see what equipment is required.

Make reasonable estimates of the amount of material to be stored on the server. Consider the number of simultaneous users, remembering peak times of the term. Also consider the institutional infrastructure and what restrictions and compatibility issues should be considered. Look carefully at the types of electronic reserve files and determine whether to offer audiovisual files or text and image files only. Consult with colleagues and campus computing services.

3. SOFTWARE

3.1 What is the best user interface for electronic reserves?

Any interface that facilitates getting the readings as quickly as possible will be the best one for your user community. The interface should provide the best possible indexing of the materials and clear instructions regarding the system's functions, including printing functions. It should deliver the reserve readings themselves in as many formats as possible. It should provide an accurate and readable screen image, downloading to hard drive or diskette and printing.

The best interface for staff will facilitate easy management of files, including entering and indexing of each file. It should provide statistical information on the use of the system and features for dealing with restrictions imposed by copyright considerations. It may be desirable for the interface to provide direct faculty access to their courses so they can update information instantly from remote locations.

3.2 Does everyone use the Web to deliver materials?

Not necessarily. However, web browsers are almost omnipresent and can allow access to the readings from almost anywhere in the world, as long as the servers are up and running. Unless your institution has built an easily accessible interface to your networking capabilities, it may be most sensible to take advantage of the web protocols.

3.2.1 Are there special issues involved with web delivery?

Copyright issues arise when there is distribution of copies. The World Wide Web is no exception. The next section, Operations Policies and Procedures, contains several questions related to a web-based electronic reserve interface.

If faculty use large graphics files, students who have modem access to the Web from remote locations may have access problems.

3.3 What sort of scanning software should I use?

Use scanning software that will produce adequate files. Base the decision on what your user community will be able to use most easily. Files that are too big, files that are hard to print, and files that are hard to read are all problems to be avoided. Many libraries have found that trying to scan with optical character recognition presents huge difficulties in quality control. Editing time is unreasonable. They have chosen instead to produce image files. Difficulties in file size can be encountered in producing image files, so it is appropriate to test software for compression capabilities and to consider what average file size is best for reserve readings. Users who are interested in downloading and printing will want files that are easy to transmit or will fit on diskettes or don't choke buffers.

3.3.1 Do I need backups?

It's always smart to back up software at every level, and electronic reserves is no exception. Once the scanning is done, it will be practical to keep backup copies of all files. Each institution will have different policies regarding backups, so it is appropriate to incorporate electronic reserves into any current system backup procedures. In-library manual backups are also appropriate in case your system is down. It might be worthwhile to consider cost/benefit ratios for this type of backup.

3.4 What indexes are libraries creating for electronic reserves?

Some libraries develop very MARC-like or actual full MARC records to access materials by course name and course number, instructor name, and sometimes by author and title. Other libraries have systems that don't provide indexes for author and title so that the database does not appear to be an electronic publication method for general access. Since readings are for specific courses, it makes the most sense to organize at least one index in that way. Some libraries also provide lists by academic department.

3.5 Are there software standards for electronic reserves?

No software standards have been developed for electronic reserves at this time.

4. OPERATIONS POLICIES AND PROCEDURES

4.1 How much does e-reserves cost?

With the rate of change in prices, it would not be helpful to attach prices in a publication such as this, but there are common components in reserve systems that should be included in any price estimate:

Equipment and furniture
- network server large enough to handle the volume of reserve traffic
- workstation equipment for each staff member (common web workstations)
- scanner equipment that will handle the volume or reserve scanning (you usually get what you pay for, so scanner prices can vary)
- tables and chairs for equipment and staff

Software

- server software
- electronic reserve software
- scanning software, which may require compression options

Staffing

- It may be possible to develop electronic reserve systems with current staff by replacing print reserve services with electronic reserves. A close examination of the various vendors offering electronic reserve services and consideration of designing an in-house system will result in different staffing needs.

4.2 Is there a union database I can use to obtain electronic files for reserves?

No, as of now there is no such database. That's probably because many bibliographic database vendors are beginning to offer full-text service for articles. Publishers are not organized to distribute single articles to users in that way at this time, and libraries are loath to spend the overhead to develop such a huge undertaking. If you are an entrepreneur with lots of time on your hands, this could be the opportunity for you.

4.2.1 Can I link to full-text resources from my electronic reserve system?

Most existing electronic reserve systems provide the function of linking to full text as well as serving full-text files.

4.3 How can I obtain electronic reserve files?

Some libraries get files from faculty members, some create files by providing scanning/reformatting services, and others use files from commercial sources. At one point in the early years of electronic reserves, there was discussion of a database that could be shared, but it has never come about. Some libraries include World Wide Web links to sites that provide full-text resources.

4.4 Who does the scanning for electronic reserves?

Many libraries provide scanning services, and several provide only the indexing software and interface for electronic reserves, leaving it up to faculty members to provide materials in electronic formats.

The libraries that offer scanning and reformatting services use a variety of staffing configurations. Many have found it necessary to write specifications for the types of files that will be accepted for electronic reserves. To get a good picture of who is scanning and their policies and procedures regarding scanning, look at several electronic reserve systems that are listed on the Electronic Reserves Clearinghouse: Links and Materials on the Web: www.mville.edu/Administration/staff/Jeff_Rosedale.

4.5 What policies and procedures documentation is important for e-reserves?

The following policy and procedure items appear in electronic reserve services policy statements and instruction pages on the World Wide Web:

- Who is eligible to use the system
- How to gain access to the system
- Description of the system and what it does
- Submission procedures or policies for electronic reserve files
- Format restrictions/specifications for electronic reserve files
- Creation of directory structure of electronic reserve files
- The extent of control faculty have over the organization of materials, such as using folders
- Technical support that is available for faculty
- Technical support that is available for students
- Server or system maintenance schedule or other information that might interfere with system use
- Duration of time electronic reserve files will remain on the system
- Fees for access or copies
- Explanations of multi-library campus situations
- Staff contact information

- Links to further information, including general library policies or copyright policies
- Paper copy availability for students
- Reserve room information for traditional reserves
- Other (campus computing support services, electronic reserve clearinghouse page)

4.6 Will there be lots of printing problems to solve?

Some printing problems are the result of file size. Testing files on various printers around campus or asking staff or students to test files on their home systems is probably a good idea.

Some printing problems are the result of the nature of the materials (e.g., color, white-on-black, screen images that do not translate to print, etc.). It is prudent to inform faculty of files that will be problematic as you develop expertise with printing problems. The reference staff in the library has encountered just about every possible printing problem, so generating a list of potentially troublesome files might not be difficult. Faculty may wish to test print files on a number of systems before submitting them to electronic reserves.

Printing prices must be resolved if your campus has not developed standard pricing policies.

4.7 Will I have to maintain a database?

Some systems use database software and some use directory structures for the files with pointers in the interface to those files. If the system is developed in-house, you may have input. Investigate vendor systems to determine which ones employ databases.

4.8 Who requests copyright permission?

Some libraries have developed permission procedures and do all permissions in-house, and some have copyright centers that take on the responsibility. Many libraries do not request permission to use materials but consider electronic reserves a fair use. The arl-ereserve discussion group archives contain many discussions regarding copyright and permissions; go to www.cni.org/Hforums/arl-ereserve/.

Electronic reserves will provide the same challenges of timeliness that print reserves present. Faculty members often bring in materials extemporaneously for the class to read and want them put on the electronic reserve system immediately. Any policies regarding copyright permission should take these faculty needs into account.

4.9 Are there guidelines to create copyright policies for electronic reserves?

Proposed CONFU (Conference on Fair Use) guidelines: www.mville.edu/Administration.staff/Jeff_Rosedale/guidelines.htm. Guidelines exist, but there is no consensus on their acceptance, so they hold no official status.

4.9.1 Is there a model e-reserves copyright policy?

The ALA model policy (www.cni.org/docs/infopols/ALA.html#mpup) was published in 1982.

4.10 How can I get information on copyright issues with electronic reserves?

The cni-copyright list is an ongoing discussion of copyright issues, and the archives are located at www.cni.org/Hforums/cni-copyright/ or from the CNI document on retrieving archives via Unix-listproc.

You can retrieve monthly logs of all arl-ereserve postings through the Unix-listproc system, but they are often relatively large files, and finding specific information within them isn't always easy.

Archives of each list are made once a month. The filename of the archive always takes the form YYMMM (where YY is the last two digits of the year and MMM is the three-character abbreviation for the name of the month). For example, the February 1994 archives are stored as a file called 94FEB. To retrieve the files via e-mail, you should send a GET command (as an e-mail note) to the address listproc@cni.org. The syntax is: GET <listname> <filename>. In this case, GET ARL-ERESERVE 94FEB. To see a list of any files associated with the archives of any particular list, you can send an INDEX command (as an e-mail note) to the address listproc@cni.org.

Peter Donovan was kind enough to provide a discussion paper on copyright for electronic reserves at the University of Pittsburgh in 1994. It's available at ftp://ftp.pitt.edu/dept/nisg/ecr/. Choose ecrcopyr.txt. The document is available in Word for Windows 2.0, in plain text (but it looks a bit tacky with the imperfect translation from Word), and in PostScript.

4.11 How should copyright policies and procedures be managed?

Most libraries seem to be managing copyright policies and procedures for electronic reserves in much the same manner as for print reserves. The policies should be made clear to faculty members and students. They should be consistent with any existing policies and procedures of the institution.

Policies should reflect the willingness to provide services with copyright-protected items and should specify the basis on which decisions will be made to enter something into the system. All policies should be reviewed periodically and should include statements about the review process, who will do the review, and the frequency of review.

4.12 Should I charge users for electronic reserves? What about prices?

Most libraries at this time do not charge fees for electronic reserves services. The libraries that do charge fees charge based on royalty fees that they are paying publishers and recovery costs for copies.

5. STAFFING

5.1 What sort of staff can provide electronic reserves?

Staff to maintain the reserve system hardware and software may include a part-time programmer as well as staff to maintain a network server for part of their time. There should be adequate staff allocated to keep track of the need for upgrades and backups and to perform those functions. If the electronic reserve system must interface with another infrastructure, staff will be needed to maintain that connection. Libraries currently use in-house library staff as well as staff from parent institutions to perform system acquisition, configuration, and maintenance functions. It is possible to buy many of the services from electronic reserve vendors, so a thorough review of what each vendor provides may help in determining staffing needs. Electronic reserve vendors can estimate how much staff time is necessary for adequate maintenance of their systems.

Public service functions that will require staff include:

Receiving and reformatting

Receiving and reformatting staff will have to receive materials from users, keep accurate records of the materials, operate reformatting equipment (scanners), perform quality control functions, and write and update policies. These processes are not unlike common print reserve functions of receiving materials, making photocopies, and processing materials for circulation. Many of the operations are routine and can be accomplished by well-trained and responsible students.

Policies and procedures should be developed with the oversight of a librarian or other permanent staff who have general knowledge of library operations and can edit and develop policies as needed. A knowledgeable and diplomatic librarian or permanent staff member should troubleshoot for problematic materials and manage the queue of materials during peak periods. The traditional peak periods for print reserve operations will probably be the peak periods for reformatting services.

Uploading and maintaining course readings and interface

It is prudent to consider who has access to functions of uploading and changing the interface; however, many uploading and interface maintenance operations become routine and can be accomplished by trained and accurate clerical or student staff. These functions are close in nature to entering bibliographic data for reserve readings into the OPAC or circulation system.

Policies and procedures for adding and deleting materials, making corrections and adjustments, and solving problems should be created and reviewed regularly with the oversight of a librarian or other permanent staff.

Public information, publicity, user support

Publicity for electronic reserve services should be accurate and meet with standards set by the library for publicity and public relations. User questions should receive timely and accurate responses. Both students and faculty will have questions concerning use of the system. Providing information for off-campus access may be necessary. Faculty will have questions concerning submission of materials and copyright restrictions.

5.2 Can the staff working on electronic reserves also manage paper reserves?

This has been the case in many libraries because print reserve services are gradually being replaced by electronic reserve services. The services and the processing routines designed to support circulation of print materials will disappear, and staff who performed those functions should be reassigned. Reformatting by scanning is somewhat like photocopying. Entering descriptions of electronic reserve items is somewhat like entering descriptions of print reserve items. Handling electronic documents and files is not really like handling paper or refilling paper, so that is one function that could require significant staff training. Public information questions about use of the system, access to the system (from remote locations), and submission of materials can probably be handled by staff members who have been providing public information for print reserves.

5.3 What efficiencies can be gained by combining paper and electronic reserve functions?

Unless completely different materials are placed in the two different kinds of reserves, circulation will go down dramatically when items are placed in the electronic reserve system. Circulation staff duties will probably be reduced. Processing tasks for print reserves may be significantly reduced. Staff time currently used to photocopy articles for faculty or to create file folders may be reduced or eliminated.

5.4 Which library department manages electronic reserves?

The print reserve department usually manages electronic reserves. It is also possible that the circulation department or access services may handle electronic reserves. Since electronic reserves may involve reformatting services as well as public information services, it is wise to consider which departments may handle these functions.

6. USER SERVICES

6.1 What sort of publicity and promotion concerns should I have?

Electronic reserve services should be clearly defined for both faculty and students. Many libraries have provided as much information as possible via their library web pages.

Faculty should be aware that there is a new service and how to access it. The web pages may not be the best way to advertise, so common or successful vehicles for getting messages to faculty should be employed.

Students should be aware of how to get to course readings. Messages that explain how to access print reserves should include as much information as possible about electronic reserves.

Explaining availability and access or "how to" information for both faculty and students is paramount. Remember that both faculty and student users may be remote and any information that is issued solely in print may be worthless.

There may be requirements for accessing electronic reserves that apply equally to accessing any services of the institution. Information that helps in connecting to campus networks, outlines equipment requirements, and explains the peculiarities of a software configuration will help remote users get to electronic reserves.

6.2 What's the best way to provide user education for electronic reserves?

Many libraries have successfully provided thorough and practical information right at the point of use in the pages of the electronic reserve system itself. Traditional user education venues such as workshops, class visits, and handouts at public service points should all be considered.

6.3 What new printing issues will arise because of electronic reserves?

Prepare pubic service staff to help users with large full-text files and standards for file formats to allow for printing. Students will likely need considerable help with printing files. Faculty members will have to understand the effects of file format and file size on printing.

In-library printing capacity may be sorely taxed by electronic reserve printing needs. Although electronic reserve printing may not differ much from usual web use, the quantity may affect printing facilities and the need to manage them.

6.4 How can I assess user satisfaction?

Make sure the system provides use statistics and monitor the statistics. Typical library assessment instruments such as the user survey should be attempted to gain insight as well. It may be most practical to develop an online survey or to engage faculty in conducting user surveys. At least one institution has conducted a telephone survey to obtain the best response rate. Evaluations have been recorded in the arl-ereserve archives, www.cni.org/Hforums/arl-ereserve/.

7. VENDORS

7.1 Who sells electronic reserve systems?

Electronic Reserves Clearinghouse: Links and Materials on the Web (www.mville.edu/Administration/staff/Jeff_Rosedale) offers a list of vendors who sell reserves systems and related products, which will likely be the best list to consult. Links are provided from the clearinghouse page to vendor web pages. Some vendors provide stand-alone systems and some offer electronic reserve modules as part of comprehensive library systems.

NOTE

1. John Kupersmith, "Definitions," e-mail to the arl-ereserve electronic discussion list (arl-ereserve@cni.org), May 5, 1994.

2

Staffing Issues
for Electronic Reserves

STEVEN J. SCHMIDT

In the final decade of the nineteenth century, American academic libraries developed the concept of special "reserved" collections as a means for ensuring the availability of high-demand items such as course readings. These collections came to be known as academic reserves or just, more typically, reserves. Materials in these reserved collections circulated for a very short period, typically just two to four hours in the building. While these collections did increase the availability of these items, it also created a number of other problems.

The high turnover of these materials made the reserve collection very labor-intensive for libraries. The constant cycle of materials being pulled from the files, checked out to the users, then returned, checked back in, and refiled required the dedication of a large number of man-hours. Since any item could be in any of a half dozen different steps at any one time, it frequently led to a loss of control within these collections. The high demand for these materials also created long lines as hordes of students competed for the limited resources. These lines often had just the opposite effect from the one the system was intended to produce. Students were constantly vying for the scarce materials, so the typical solution was to add extra copies to the reserve collection, which just added to the staff's burden.

Over a century later these reserve processes have been automated, but the fundamental problems of this type of operation are still around.

This fact becomes even more frightening when you consider the complexity of maintaining this type of system coupled with the sheer volume of materials involved today.

In the last decade, most academic libraries have turned to computer and web-based technology as the solution. In its most common incarnation, the electronic reserve process consists of converting print copies of the course readings to an electronic file format that is accessible over the Internet or campus network. An electronic reserve collection differs dramatically from a paper-based one and usually benefits both sides of the circulation desk.

THE PAPER-BASED PARADIGM

Consider the model of the traditional paper-based reserve desk.

A student comes up to the desk and asks for the class readings. Sometimes students have checked a catalog to see what's available, but they usually just ask. If the requested material is available, the clerk at the desk retrieves it from the files and checks it out to the student. The student is then free to review the material for a short time or to photocopy it, as most students do. The student then returns the material to the clerk at the desk, who checks it back in and refiles it.

Multiply this process by the number of students in a class and you have a very labor-intensive process. Multiply that figure by the number of classes being taught that semester and you have a staffing and workflow nightmare.

Exact figures don't exist on the amount of time spent searching for misfiled items and on time spent repairing or reorganizing worn or damaged materials, but common sense and experience tell us that they are substantial. Students as a rule are more interested in getting a copy of the reading for themselves than they are in maintaining the original in good condition for the next user. At least one library reported that when it used a paper reserve system, that system accounted for less than one-quarter of the library's total circulation but generated more than three-quarters of all complaints and problems.[1]

ELECTRONIC RESERVES PARADIGM

According to Laura Gasaway, it was "only natural for libraries to turn to technology to solve a variety of problems caused by reserve collections. First of all, reserve collections occupy considerable space and are not easy to manage. Second, because the individual photocopied items are unbound pieces, they have to be placed in folders or some other cover to prevent loss and to keep them with other reserve items for that course. . . . Third, because faculty members tend to reuse items, the library often has to photocopy the material each semester as the copies are worn, marked on, etc. Fourth, the items have to be checked out and back in as users retrieve and use them. Lastly, the library has to determine what to do with the items at the end of the semester."[2]

Every minute spent scanning and linking materials to a web-based reserve system reduces the amount of time your frontline staff will have to spend fetching, filing, and refiling paper reserve materials. An electronic system also eliminates the loss or damage of reserve materials, since each user gets a clean, complete, and collated copy. Finally, electronic reserves extend the availability of your collection to your clientele far beyond the physical boundaries and hours of your facility.

Consider the basic paradigm of an electronic reserve system:

> Instead of queuing up to the reserve desk, students now just need to access the reserve system from any Internet capable computer. They are no longer dependent upon the limited hours of the library, nor do they even have to be physically in the facility since most electronic reserve systems can be accessed from any computer on campus or, in a growing number of cases, attached to the Internet. Each student receives a complete set of the readings without torn, scrambled, or missing pages. Depending upon the system, the student may read, print, or download the materials for later study.

What impact does this scenario have on the circulation desk? First of all, it can mean a substantial reduction in the demand upon the staff at the circulation desk. The desk clerks no longer have to spend a large part of their day facing long lines of impatient students. Gone is the repetitive loop of finding, checking out, checking in, and refiling reserve materials. Gone, too, is the need to spend time and resources searching for misplaced materials or repairing and replacing worn materials.

BACKROOM OPERATIONS—PROCESSING RESERVES

Just as the real benefit of an electronic reserve system is shared between the user and the frontline staff, the true cost lies in the backroom operation.

No matter which system your institution uses, paper or electronic, processing reserve materials is a laborious undertaking. While electronic access will lessen the confusion and staff load at the public desk, it typically adds several steps to the backroom workflow.

Based upon a review of the literature and an informal survey of a small number of libraries, it is obvious that there is very little standardization in the way libraries process for reserves. This is not surprising since most electronic reserve processes are outgrowths and expansions of paper-based systems, but it makes it difficult to make sweeping statements about workflow. However, most paper-based operations include these basic steps:

1. Instructor submits materials for reserve.
2. Library processes materials for circulation.
3. Library processes copyright clearance.
4. Library files materials for access.
5. Library makes materials available for checkout.
6. Students request materials at desk.
7. Library retrieves materials.
8. Library checks materials out to student.
9. Student uses materials.
10. Student returns materials to desk.
11. Library files materials.
12. Repeat steps 6–11.

Some libraries process all materials as if they were going to circulate them over the counter. This is necessary because not everything submitted for reserves is suitable for electronic access. When the University of North Carolina went into production with its electronic reserve system, it intended to integrate all eligible reserves into the electronic system, but this decision raised several issues.[3] Complete books, for example, are not usually mounted electronically because they present copyright concerns as well as online storage and printing issues, and because very large items are difficult to scan in a timely fashion. These institutions create a circulation record for each item and often an OPAC (online public access catalog) entry. Then selected items are set aside for scanning.

A growing number of reserve systems are linking directly to full-text articles in locally licensed databases rather than to locally scanned and mounted copies. On the surface, this appears to be the easiest and most cost-effective solution for libraries because all this process requires is a link to the article's URL. Linking preserves image quality, eliminates the need for scanning, and is usually permitted under the database licenses and section 107 of the Copyright Act of 1976.

On the downside, many databases still lack graphics or a unique "linkable" URL for each individual article. Also, a number of database providers require a separate password in order to access the article, which makes using these links difficult for the end user. However, the main reason for the rarity of this solution appears to be the faculty. Most faculty still tend to submit a paper copy of an article rather than a link to an Internet version. This means that someone on the reserve staff has to locate a suitable online copy of the readings, assuming that a linkable version is available within that institution's licensed resources.

The Virginia Commonwealth University library has successfully integrated linking into its reserve process. The workflow includes searching for acceptable titles to which the library holds electronic subscriptions. The staff has reviewed the vendor licenses to confirm the stability of links; complete full-text, with illustrations; and permission for them to link; and created a master list of approved e-journals. As requests are processed, a staff member compares the title with this list to see if linking is a possibility.

The most common type of submission is still a photocopied journal article or book chapter. Some libraries will do the photocopying for the faculty, which ensures a clean, straight copy. Others require the instructor to provide the photocopies. In this situation, the quality of the materials is usually borderline to poor. From a staffing point of view, the trade-off is image quality versus the manpower to photocopy a mass of material in a timely fashion.

Let's turn now to the processing paradigm for electronic reserves. In this scenario most of the labor is focused on the later half, the public end, of the process. The scenario starts out with a pattern that is very similar to the one used to process paper-based reserves, but it includes only the backroom functions. Once the materials are mounted on the server, all access falls outside the reserve desk operation. In most electronic reserve operations the workflow goes something like this:

1. Instructor submits materials for reserve.
2. Library processes materials for scanning.
3. Library processes copyright clearance.
4. Library scans and mounts materials on server.

The biggest variable involves the amount of preprocessing each individual institution chooses to do. As previously mentioned, there is very little standardization. One of the most common patterns found today is the review of all of the materials submitted by the faculty for reserves on a case-by-case basis. In this situation, a library staff member will evaluate each item to see whether it can be mounted electronically within that library's interpretation of the fair-use guidelines. Typically, the person making this decision is a clerical person working with a set of criteria rather than a copyright expert.

When the University of North Carolina decided to take on the management of copyright compliance, it found that its current reserve forms didn't provide enough information to request clearances.[4] This meant that many requests had to be completed by the staff or returned to the instructors for completion. This created a large backlog in processing. One possible solution was to hire a number of temporary workers to get through the backlog, but neither funds nor staff were available.

The criteria used for copyright review will vary greatly. Currently, most libraries appear to be limiting the documents placed on electronic reserves to items that do not present copyright complications. This saves the libraries from paying the royalties needed for mounting copyrighted materials but typically restricts the readings to materials created by the instructor, such as lecture notes and syllabi, or to materials that are obviously in the public domain, such as government documents.

Over a century ago, long before the advent of photocopiers and electronic reserves, Mark Twain wrote, "There is one thing [that is] impossible for God, and that is to make sense out of any copyright law in existence."[5] The interpretation of copyright law can be very complicated and is best left to the lawyers. However, sidestepping the copyright issue by putting up only royalty-free materials may not be the best service the library can provide to its students.

No matter how it chooses to deal with copyright, the best move a library can make is to align itself with its institution's attorneys. A growing number of libraries today are doing just that and are going to the other extreme by considering all reserve material to be fair game for electronic access. For these organizations, a close working relationship between the reserve staff and the institution's copyright attorneys is a must.

One case where this arrangement has worked successfully is the IUPUI (Indiana University-Purdue University Indianapolis) University

Library. The IUPUI University Library houses the Indiana University Copyright Management Center. Headed by Kenneth Crews, the center advises faculty and staff on how to deal with copyright issues.[6] The center worked closely with the library staff to distill a small set of guidelines that allow the staff to deal with copyright issues in a timely fashion. These guidelines outline when and how a particular item can be made available electronically. This information empowers a staff member to make case-by-case decisions on 90 percent of the materials submitted. The remaining ones are referred to the Copyright Management Center for a final decision.

Precise record keeping is also a vital and complicated part of reserve processing. In a typical situation, there are two types of records kept. First, all of the relevant bibliographic and course data are entered into a database as materials are processed and scanned. A staff member then sorts this database to identify materials that require permission. Most permissions are funneled though the Copyright Clearance Center (CCC), which is the largest clearinghouse for obtaining permission, but a number of requests are sent directly to the copyright holder.

The second half of this process involves keeping track of the charges and payments made for clearances. Currently, most libraries are picking up these charges, but a few are billing the royalty charges back to the individual department. The cost of requesting this type of clearance is not cheap, but it must be weighed against the convenience and service the library provides to students.

There is an enduring myth that modern technology will save us both time and money. This is rarely the case. Electronic reserves are very expensive operations in terms of both technology and manpower, and once the die is cast, there is no going back. The value of such a system cannot be measured in terms of what it costs, but rather in the service it provides. Properly implemented, an electronic reserve system can greatly enhance the availability of the resources your students need. The trade-off is relatively low-end staff on the front end of an inefficient and labor-intensive process versus staff with specialized skills in the backroom who provide a popular and on-demand service to your users.

NOTES

1. IUPUI University Library, Smithsonian Case Study: Errol (Electronic Reserves @ University Library). November 1999. May 25, 2001, at <http://errol.iupui.edu/Laureate/casestudy.htm>.

2. Laura N. Gasaway, "Library Reserve Collections: From Paper to Electronic Collections," in *Growing Pains: Adapting Copyright for Libraries, Education, and Society* (Littleton, Colo.: Fred Rothman, 1997), 141.

3. Leah G. McGinnis, "Electronic Reserves at the University of North Carolina: Milestones and Challenges in Implementing a New Service," *Journal of Interlibrary Loan, Document Delivery & Information Supply* 9(4) (1999): 73–85.

4. Ibid.

5. "Mark Twain on Copyright Law," *New York Times*, December 25, 1881, quoted in *Mark Twain Speaks for Himself,* ed. Paul Fatout (West Lafayette, Ind.: Purdue Univ. Pr., 1978), 132.

6. Kenneth D. Crews, Electronic Reserves and Copyright at IUPUI, at www.iupui.edu/~copyinfo/ereserves.html, April 24, 2000.

3

Evaluation of Electronic Reserve Systems

BUD HILLER

In the mid-1990s, libraries across the country began investigating the possibility of digitizing their reserve collections. Tempting as the thought of getting rid of file cabinets full of scraggly, faded photocopies may have been, administrators were quickly stumped by two major obstacles. The first barrier was the difficulty of scanning a collection of thousands of articles into a workable electronic format, and the second was the trickiness of creating an easily used but stable system by which students and faculty could gain access to these many digital files. Other chapters in this book will touch upon the scanning aspects of creating electronic reserves. This chapter examines some of the variables in determining whether to purchase or write an electronic reserve system and in evaluating how the system is working on your campus.

BUY OR WRITE?

Colleges and universities are filled with students and staff who can write Perl, ASP, and CGI scripts; create databases; write HTML or use WYSIWYG software like Macromedia's Dreamweaver or Adobe's PageMill; and configure a web server on Unix or NT. At these schools, the immediate thought must be that there is no need to purchase an electronic reserve system because all of the components are in place to write one using campus expertise and facilities. Although the school faces the prospect of reinventing the wheel when it comes to writing and serving the appropriate software, the institution benefits by having a customized system specifically designed to meet the needs of on-campus users. E-reserve systems can cost thousands of dollars. Perhaps students or staff can put together the framework of a system for little or no additional cost.

Questions to Ask

But writing a working system for electronic reserves is no small task and should not be undertaken without a full exploration of other options. While it may be possible to create a system that offers a clear method of storing electronic materials and an efficient process for retrieving them, maintaining that system has to be a key consideration as well. Some questions that might arise include:

1. Who will write the system? If staff will be assigned the task, who will perform their other duties? If students, who will monitor, understand, and maintain their work once they leave campus?
2. Who will oversee the system so that the programmers' work will integrate with the people creating the electronic files and the servers that will distribute them?
3. How elaborate a system does the institution require? Will a simple listing of courses and materials suffice, or is a more complete (and complicated) system desired?
4. What technology will be used to create the system? Will a home-cooked set of advanced scripts and codes with the latest updated languages work from the outset, or will the institution depend upon a more tried-and-true older set of programs at first?
5. How will the system be updated as needs change through the years?

Benefits of Writing Your Own System

If a university examines these questions and determines that an on-campus design is indeed possible, it can take advantage of some of the benefits that custom creation can offer. For example, if a staff member is designated as the All-Knowing Creator and Maintainer of the system, service can be immediate. Rather than calling or e-mailing a technical support team in the case of a problem, the reserve administrator can call a colleague down the hall who has this homegrown system as his or her top priority. If the administrator envisions a certain feature that will work well on this campus, the staff member who maintains the system can immediately write out new scripts. The system can incorporate all of the fonts, colors, and design of the campus web pages in order to make the e-reserve system fit more seamlessly within the overall framework of the institution. The school doesn't have to pay for features it doesn't need. For example, if a school doesn't care about copyright management, the system doesn't need to include those features.

Benefits of Purchasing a System

On the other hand, a school might look at these questions and decide that other people with more knowledge and time might be better positioned to offer an electronic reserve system for a price. In some circumstances, it might be a realization that outsourcing work to companies that specialize in certain products is sometimes a more efficient way to offer services. In other cases, people with the necessary expertise might not exist on staff, or those individuals who have the knowledge may be transitory (students are the classic example of short-term, low-cost, temporary workers).

Rather than start from scratch on writing a system that may or may not work within a designated time frame, a school might invest in a system that is known to work and that can be installed quickly. In this case, the school will have to realize an up-front cost for the purchase of the product and maintenance contracts, which may seem to be more expensive than simply using the skill sets of existing staff. But the writing and support of a complicated system can eat up enormous amounts of time for well-compensated computer-literate personnel on a campus, which may make a homegrown system more expensive over time. A purchased system usually offers a support team that may be more available than a single on-campus individual, who may be on vacation, sabbatical, leave, or a job hunt elsewhere when things go wrong. Purchased systems usually offer regular version updates as they respond to improvement requests from institutions across the country and can often suggest which sets of software and hardware might be needed to run the system correctly.

Summary of the Buy/Write Decision Process

In the end, an institution needs to weigh the options of purchasing or writing its electronic reserves system. Rather than thinking of it as a "buy/write" question, the school should rephrase it as a "buy right" process. With either option, a school is going to invest thousands of dollars, so it is important to look at the advantages of each setup and invest in the right one for the needs of its end users: the students and faculty at the school.

EVALUATING A SYSTEM ONCE IT IS IN PLACE

In any electronic reserve system, evaluation takes place at many levels. First, the school must evaluate its users' needs to determine if electronic reserves is a desired option. If the choice is made to pursue this option, the administration must explore choices regarding purchasing a self-contained, off-the-shelf product or creating a customized package of on-campus pages to deliver the digitized files. Once this choice has been made and the reserve room has been transformed into a virtual location where students and faculty can access required readings electronically over the Web from many locations across campus, the college or university must examine how well the system is working. Before it can determine how successful the system is at its primary function of delivering electronic files, the school should expand its definition of success.

First Glance—How Is the System Working?

When driving a car, speed kills. When driving a computer, the *lack* of speed kills. An electronic reserve system has to respond quickly to a user's request for a document. The user has to be able to maneuver easily through a system, find what is needed, retrieve it on screen, and send it to the printer without waiting more than a few seconds for each command to complete. So the first test should be a test of speed—if the system consistently takes longer than a few seconds on any one of these steps, additional fine-tuning may be necessary.

Before a user retrieves a document, however, he or she has to be able to find it. Cross-referencing material by department, by instructor, by course, or even by title or author may be necessary to ensure that even a novice user with little experience and no training could follow links to the required material. Electronic reserve systems are set up to be used by thousands of students and faculty, many of whom are let loose on the Web without instruction. They are given a vague directive: Find that article on e-reserves and read it for tomorrow's class. A successful system will be clearly linked to a logical portal and will clearly present the steps a user must take. Naturally, there should be no hidden steps or shortcuts that an experienced user could take advantage of but that a newbie might never stumble across. In e-reserves, as in traditional reserves, there is nothing more frustrating to a staff member than to put forth extra effort to make material available for a faculty member who waited to the last minute and then to discover that users can't find the item in time for the class.

If the system responds quickly most of the time, and users find it easy to use, the collection of courses online should increase. The number and variety of faculty users should also increase. Over time, if the system is working well, electronic reserves will play a larger and more permanent role in the way faculty teach their courses. A quick evaluation at this point will indicate that electronic reserves has been a success. But there are additional, deeper factors at play here that may provide insights into other methods by which the system might be evaluated.

Student Evaluation of an Electronic Reserve System

Because students are the primary beneficiaries of a system that digitizes material and allows users to bypass the traditional "charge out at the reserve desk and make a photocopy" method of obtaining reserve readings, student evaluations of electronic reserves are key. The feedback from this group can drive the system forward or sink it altogether, depending upon how well the students perceive it. In many instances, an absence of complaints equals success, as students don't have the same long-term institutional memory that staff and faculty have. For a first- or second-year student, electronic reserves may be all he or she has ever known, so naturally there will not be an onslaught of comparative compliments along the lines of "this is so much better than the old way." The students expect the system to work well, and only a disruption in service will bring about a (negative) reaction.

Positive student notice can be determined by whether students recommend that faculty place reserve materials for class on e-reserves. If faculty arrive at the reserve desk with only a vague notion of what e-reserves might be, but with an idea that their students have recommended it and might benefit by it, then the students have judged e-reserves to be an effective method of operating.

Students often adjust to change more quickly than staff or faculty and are willing to bounce around a site in order to find material, but they are less willing to wait for materials to display or print. Even ten seconds seems an eternity for students used to instant access, and a file size that extends beyond a megabyte might take several minutes to print on an older printer with 4MB or less of memory. A student evaluating electronic reserves might be more interested in how fast a document loaded and printed than in such factors as the quality of the print.

Time Savings for Students

Any evaluation of electronic reserves has to involve time savings, and sometimes it is difficult for students to realize how much time a smoothly operating e-reserve system might save. Students might not remember heading to the library in all weather, day or night, standing in line to see if material is available at the reserve desk, and then standing in line again and paying to photocopy that material. Even the slowest server and the most poorly written search scripts will provide quicker service over the course of a semester than the most efficient traditional reserve system. Ten seconds to load and a minute to print a document that is available twenty-four hours a day and is never missing crucial pages is not a long time to wait. But as students get more used to research materials being available online, an evaluation of time savings has to go beyond comparing traditional reserves and electronic reserves—it has to compare various methods of electronic access.

For example, many libraries now subscribe to a number of online databases. These resources provide fast, full-text access to a wide variety of articles, but, unfortunately, most have their own peculiarities with regard to searching and finding these articles. A way to measure the effectiveness of an electronic reserve system would be to see if it aids the student in quickly finding and printing articles from all these different databases. If the system allows a faculty member to place many links on a single e-reserve page, giving students access to many articles but requiring them to remember how to find only one page location, then it has succeeded in saving time for students.

Faculty Evaluation of an Electronic Reserve System

Faculty members have a different set of expectations for an electronic reserve system. Many professors are less used to the multiple-click world that students live in and so are less likely to use a system that does not provide a clear and logical progression of steps in order to access materials. Some of the usual shortcuts that experienced users take for granted might be lost on a faculty member who has only recently embraced the advantages of technology. "Clarity lost, coolness gained" is not a positive trade-off for faculty, nor is any site that requires nonstandard plug-ins, sound cards, or only the latest and greatest browser update. On a related note, faculty members are less likely to put up with a smudged or unclear scan of material, preferring instead to wait a little longer for a better quality image to display and print. Finally, while many faculty are thrilled with the possibilities that e-reserves can offer, the bottom line is always going to be availability. If the material takes too long to process, if the server is down too frequently, or if students complain that they were not able to find or print their assigned readings, it will be back to the traditional reserve room for faculty and back to the drawing board for the reserve room staff.

Some methods by which faculty can positively evaluate the system include word-of-mouth recommendations to each other, direct feedback to the e-reserve administrator, and indirect feedback to the overall supervisor of e-reserves. Another way in which they can evaluate a system is to determine whether students read materials that are available electronically more regularly than they read materials that can be found only in paper form at the reserve desk. Anecdotal evidence suggests that students do in fact read a higher percentage of reserve material if it is available online, a trend that will encourage faculty to continue with electronic reserves.

In addition, faculty can offer the highest evaluations of a system by actually changing their method of teaching because of the opportunities that electronic reserves can provide. For example, one of the benefits of electronic distribution of materials is that many users can access items simultaneously. A faculty member might be able to assign a class of fifteen students to turn in papers electronically on Wednesday and read all of their classmates' papers by Friday. In a traditional reserve system, it would be impossible for that many students to get a copy of each of the papers in time, but it can work in a well-run electronic environment. One of the strongest compliments for any electronic reserve system is that faculty begin taking advantage of these opportunities on a regular basis, which means they have developed full confidence that materials will be available and students will be able to find them.

Time Savings for Faculty

While faculty members might not realize the same sort of savings a student might, their evaluation of an electronic reserve system will hinge in part on whether it will take more or less time for them to place materials on e-reserves than it does to place them on traditional reserves. If it will take considerably longer for electronic reserves to be processed than paper reserves, will faculty have to plan much further in advance (always a difficult proposition)? Will better copies have to be found and provided? Will more information be required in order to acquire copyright permission? Or, conversely, will the improved ability to link to online databases, magazine articles, and web sites require less work and less advance planning? Many faculty are extraordinarily short of time, and their evaluation of e-reserves will be based in part on whether it adds time to their day or subtracts from it.

Organization Evaluation of an Electronic Reserve System

The organization that initiated the installation of electronic reserves, whether it be the library, the computer center, or some combination of the two, will evaluate the system on many different levels. The organization will be trying to determine if its investment is paying off—are hardware, software, and personnel being used in a way that furthers the educational mission? Furthermore, the organization will be hearing and responding to the perceptions of its clients (students and faculty), improving the system as needed. Finally, the organization will view an electronic reserve system as it views so many other technological advances—as a potential area of marketing that can give it an advantage in competing for educational funding.

In fact, it is the organization, rather than the students or faculty, that realizes the most indirect benefits of a successful electronic reserve system. Students can judge a system by looking at whether materials are available online that they can access from locations all over campus. Faculty can judge whether course materials are read more frequently online or whether e-reserves makes their life easier. An organization, however, has to look beyond the personal, immediate benefits to evaluate the system.

A successful electronic reserve system represents a true collaboration among staff, faculty, and students. The development of a system creates a sense of community among the stakeholders—the groups have a vested interest in working together to create a system that works well for all involved. For example, faculty members who worked closely with the staff to solve problems of layout and presentation of reserve materials have developed a trust and respect for the staff. Students who worked within groups and submitted articles for e-reserves have been able to see firsthand the work that goes into creating an efficient system and have come to appreciate the fact that their materials are more accessible and convenient. These types of successful interactions improve the relationships involved, and faculty and students can look forward to further successful projects. Any evaluation of an e-reserve system has to take into account this effective interaction among the diverse elements of a university. For the organization that initiated this collaboration, a successful e-reserve system can pay dividends years down the road.

In addition, a technologically advanced system of electronic file retrieval is a perfect fit in an environment where universities are installing networked computer access in every room. As more schools require or recommend personal computers for their students, and as more money is spent on faster modem connections, new wiring, and cross-campus wireless network access, an intranet that supplies thousands of students with classroom materials on a daily basis benefits. Very few applications so clearly exploit this technology, and few expenses can be more clearly justified to parents, students, and trustees.

Time Savings for the Organization

Saving time can be a huge benefit for the organization, but it may not be instantly recognized when an e-reserve system is evaluated. With e-reserves, as with so many other services that are expensive, questions will be raised regarding how much money and time the system will save. While a strong case could be made that, over several semesters, an institution will save both time and money with an e-reserve system, it takes a determined investigator to ferret out and communicate what these savings might be.

On first inspection, it will almost always take longer to process electronic reserves than traditional reserves. It takes more time to scan, edit, and post files than it does to put a bar code on an article, enter a quick cataloging record, and add a copyright stamp. The actual time saved comes into effect over the course of the semester. Students don't have to walk to the library to get articles. Staff members don't have to try to hunt down missing pages or lost articles. Student assistants don't have to retrieve and reshelve the same item dozens of times as the weeks go by. If computer files are archived, even the original creation of the document is only a one-time deal, so future uses of the same article might require even less time to process than traditional reserves.

In evaluating a system, one must examine how time savings translate into monetary savings. For example, if student assistants are spending considerably less time at the reserve desk tracking down the same articles and homework solution sets, perhaps they can work on other tasks, or fewer assistants might be needed. Storage space that previously was needed for paper reserve files can now be used for something else, alleviating the need to purchase extra cabinets. Rather than making multiple copies of an article for reserve room use, a photocopying department needs to make only a single copy for scanning. Over a year, this will add up to a considerable amount of time that can be spent on other work. Most schools also use automatic document feeders on their scanners, which allow other work to take place during the time-consuming parts of the processing functions.

Obviously, it is difficult to place a single dollar figure on time saved—does it equal the amount spent on new hardware and software? Does it exceed this amount? If so, by how much? Some schools may decide to realize monetary savings immediately by hiring fewer students for the reserve desk, but others may decide to reinvest that time in additional services. The latter decision may pay off several years down the line as the full-service, customer-oriented organization becomes a selling point for applicants to the institution.

SUMMARY

In evaluating whether to write a customized e-reserve system or to purchase one, an institution needs to look at both methods with a particular eye to maintenance and updates. Having a brilliant sophomore in the organization with a sharp eye for web design and an ability to tie together databases with scripts is wonderful, but three years after that student has graduated, who will be able to debug a system failure or update the system to take advantage of new technology? A complete and simple system with on-site support may provide a better solution for an institution that wants a setup that meets the organizational needs without charging for extraneous fluff.

Once an institution has a system in place, it needs to look to several locations and many levels to evaluate whether the system is doing a decent job. Students, faculty, and the organization itself will have different perspectives on what "decent" might be or how successful the operation is. In examining the success of the venture, the organization must do more than measure use statistics, the cost of the hardware and software, or the amount of processing time. When viewed over the course of the semester, electronic reserves will assuredly create huge time savings if the assessor combines the student convenience factor with the reduction in staff and reserve room maintenance issues.

But a true evaluation for the organization has to go beyond the measurement of simple efficiency. A well-run electronic reserve operation can improve the sense of community that exists in the diverse university environment. Positive interaction between staff and faculty encourages both groups to look forward to further interaction. Students who appreciate the improvement in service form deeper relationships with staff. The development of innovative technologies that take advantage of campus-wide network access allows students and faculty to connect in imaginative ways. In order to appraise the true value of an e-reserve system, an organization has to look at hard data, but, more importantly, it has to measure whether the system has reached the more esoteric goals that are the hallmark of the entire system of higher education.

4

Migrating E-Reserves to a New IOLS

M. CLAIRE DOUGHERTY

Northwestern University Library is the home of the original NOTIS (Northwestern Online Totally Integrated System) library management system and one of the early pioneers in electronic reserves. Oddly enough, however, when Northwestern mounted its first e-reserves in 1994, it was treated as a thing apart. At that time, it was managed in a gopher system, which soon became a web-based system, and it was not completely integrated with NOTIS-based print reserve management and delivery. There were sound reasons for this division, but as the volume and complexity of e-reserve requests mounted, it became apparent that some kind of integration would be necessary to relieve the tremendous burden dual systems placed on both staff and patrons. In September 1998, Northwestern successfully migrated to the Endeavor Voyager library system and completely integrated its print and electronic reserves.

Libraries starting up an e-reserve operation have many management options open to them. This chapter explores the benefits and limitations of managing e-reserves through an integrated online library system (IOLS) by looking at the Northwestern experience and discusses points on which libraries may want to focus as they plan to implement or improve existing e-reserve systems.

MIGRATING NORTHWESTERN FROM NOTIS TO VOYAGER

It seems obvious in today's information environment to suggest that any IOLS under consideration for reserve management should support clickable hyperlinks. When Northwestern began providing e-reserves in October 1994, however, the telnet-based NOTIS OPAC (online public access catalog) client did not support click-through URLs. This was the primary reason why the Electronic Reserve Task Force chose to mount the electronic reserve system (ERS) separately. With significant support from campus information technology staff on the task force, the first e-reserves were scanned and stored as image-only Adobe Acrobat PDF documents and delivered to students through a gopher menu system. Based on the success of gopher, and anticipating improved service and flexibility with the World Wide Web's HTTP protocol, the task force wrote a university special budget request for the library's first dedicated server-class Unix web server. The university awarded the money, and by late spring of 1995, ERS had migrated to the Web. Each professor's class was given its own static ERS web page listing the course materials available electronically (see fig.1). As demand was relatively light, fewer

FIGURE 1   ERS class page, circa 1996

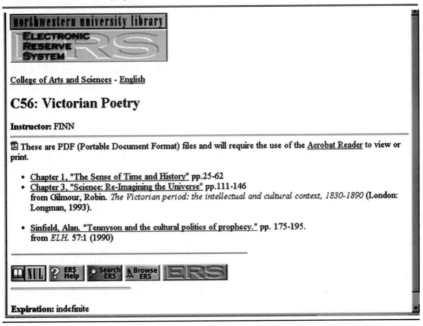

than twenty classes in the first year, this approach was manageable for a time.

In addition to creating and updating static HTML pages for each course, reserve staff managed a navigation structure built to get the student to his or her course. This tool was a series of hierarchical menus, also static HTML, in three levels: a list of schools at the university, a list of departments in each school, and a list of courses using ERS for each department. Each quarter, links were manually changed to reflect the offerings and eliminate dead-end links. The library webmaster instituted a SWISH web search engine, which, through a nightly batch job, updated any data altered on the site within the past twenty-four hours.[1] Staff in the main library's reserve services department were responsible for most of this maintenance since they produced the largest volume of e-reserves and were the only reserve unit that both used NOTIS and generated e-reserve documents. Of the three next-largest reserve units, the Schaffner Chicago campus library was not using NOTIS for print reserve, and the science and music libraries had not yet begun to offer e-reserves.

During the first two years of ERS, most faculty maintained materials in both print and electronic reserves. Entire books, of course, could be available only in print. Since the technology itself was so new, accessing excerpted materials electronically was initially optional for students, which meant a copy of each reading was also available in physical format. It was therefore necessary to place notes in both the NOTIS print system and on ERS web pages instructing users to look elsewhere for materials in other formats. It also became apparent that although URLs could not provide direct access to electronic materials, for tracking purposes (and particularly for copyright tracking) URLs would have to be included in the NOTIS reserve system records. This was the best tool available to staff for seeing, at a glance, what pieces had been scanned, which were available only in print, and the number of times each had been placed on reserve. In 1996, staff began to add URLs to the NOTIS record's 856 fields.

Because the NOTIS reserve database was isolated from the rest of the library's holdings, the staff over time fell into some fairly unorthodox cataloging practice. Since most reserve records were based, at least in some part, on existing items in the collection, standard procedure was to copy a bibliographic record from the main catalog to the reserve catalog and edit by removing all fields from 500 on, replacing them with local data. While this was to cause significant problems when the time came to migrate to the Voyager system, it did allow for some fairly specific control over reserve information. One of the original developers of NOTIS, Jim Aagaard, made significant enhancements to Northwestern's reserve module to create searchable indexes for class, quarter, instructor, and activation/deactivation dates and to print special notes in the OPAC client and on call slips. The 500 and 799 fields were used for specific reserve purposes as shown in figure 2.

Not shown in this example are two staff-only fields, the 940 field, which was used for notes pertaining to copyright status, and the 956 field, which was used to permanently store URLs. This storage field was necessary because some pieces were used in print from quarter to quarter but only occasionally in electronic format. For statistical and reactivation purposes, each URL for each piece had to be retained. Looking at this sample record, we identify another limitation of the old NOTIS system, which transcended the format of the files themselves: course, instructor, and date information were specific to the piece and had to be entered manually at the beginning of each quarter. Even with keyboard macros, this was an extremely tedious process.

Reserve staff had begun to discuss the possibility of developing an auxiliary relational or SGML-based database to automate web display of ERS data when the library announced it would search for a replacement to NOTIS. A library-wide committee, the NOTIS Replacement Task Force, was formed in late 1996 to compose an RFP and manage the selection process. Reserve staff in all branch libraries came together to compose a reserve wish list. Among the items on the list partially or

FIGURE 2   Combination print and electronic reserve record from NOTIS, circa 1997

```
LTRM DONE                                           FAE1998
NOTIS CATALOGING              LR10
RM# FAE1998 FMT B RT a BL m DT 09/18/96 R/DT 10/09/97 STAT fa E/L   DCF a D/S D
SRC    PLACE enk LANG eng MOD    I/LEV   REPRO    D/CODE s DT/1 1995 DT/2
CONT b    ILLUS         GOVT    BIOG    FEST 0 CONF 0 FICT 0 INDX 1

100:1 : |a Eagleton, Terry, |d 1943-
245:10: |a Heathcliff and the Great Hunger : |b studies in Irish culture / |c
Terry Eagleton.
260:   : |a London ; |a New York : |b Verso, |c 1995.
500/1: : |a ...2-HOUR/OVERNIGHT
500/2: : |a PORTIONS AVAILABLE ON ELECTRONIC RESERVE
799/1: : |a ENG D51; FALL 96; |b Finn |d 08/24/96 |e 12/14/96
799/2: : |a ENG C59; FALL 97; |b Finn |d 08/25/97 |e 12/15/97
856/1:0 : |a http://www.library.nwu.edu/ERS/cas/english/C59/FAE1998.pdf |d
pp.1-26
```

completely pertaining to e-reserves were public searching for reserve materials through the main OPAC (no longer a separate database for reserve), simple deactivation and reactivation of previously used reserve course records, copyright tracking, a document management system to organize and store e-reserve files, active hyperlinking to URLs for e-reserve materials, and the ability to restrict access to materials at the user level.

The last point was important for copyright reasons. Between the time Northwestern began providing e-reserves in 1994 and the time it began searching for a new system in 1996, the Conference on Fair Use (CONFU) issued its proposed copyright guidelines for electronic reserve systems, but they were never formally approved by that body.[2] The proposed guidelines recommended instituting passwords or other protections to ensure that only students in a particular class were accessing e-reserve material. There were no such protections in place with ERS. Access to documents was restricted to the Internet password addresses on the Northwestern campus network, a restriction easily circumvented by any visitor to a campus library, computer lab, classroom building, or office. The staff in the main library's reserve services department and the members of the Electronic Reserve Task Force felt that the inaccessibility of the NOTIS reserve module and its restrictive search types raised some additional barriers to unauthorized access but might prove scant protection in case of an actual lawsuit.

In December 1996, Northwestern announced that it had selected Voyager, and planning began in earnest. One of the first orders of business for reserve staff was to evaluate Endeavor's Image Server product. This tool, at the time in very early stages of production, was primarily designed for institutions new to digital document production and scanning. Its workflow tools seemed primitive compared with the relatively sophisticated Adobe Acrobat Capture product, which several reserve units at Northwestern had been using with success. Endeavor touted Image Server for its copyright management tool, which, although thorough in conception, was designed primarily to track access to materials at the user level; it was not geared to staff wishing to track use across academic periods and permissions granted by publishers. The Image Server offered no additional document management tools or storage beyond what was natively available with 856 field links to external documents in standard bibliographic records, and in fact seemed merely to be an alternative, and somewhat more limited, cataloging module. It contained no interface to the reserve functions of associating digital documents with courses and professors. Northwestern decided based on these investigations that the Image Server was not worth the additional expense.

Reserve staff moved on to planning for NOTIS reserve record migration and to designing an integrated print and electronic processing workflow for units in all branch libraries. Record migration proved to be a major undertaking and in the end was perhaps not quite worth the effort. Anticipating that faculty might return the first postmigration year requesting that their old lists be reactivated, reserve staff were anxious not to lose their historical record. Another data migration challenge was to maintain the linkage between reserve records and library bibliographic records. Under NOTIS, the process of copying a bibliographic record from the main catalog to the reserve catalog created a special field to store the NOTIS bibliographic record number. With the migration to Voyager, NOTIS bib record numbers were to be themselves converted, and thus any staff member wishing to traverse from a NOTIS reserve bib to a NOTIS main bib would be forced to perform double searches. In actual practice, this was rarely necessary. Copying records was primarily useful when entire book titles were to be placed on reserve. In these cases, the records, minus their 500+ fields, were presented in the reserve database more or less intact.

With the new Voyager system, it became possible for staff to temporarily associate items in the main collection with reserves without altering bibliographic records in any way. The less complete copies of these records from the reserve database were therefore not as useful; in fact, to use them would interfere with the ability to track items throughout the system by temporary reserve circulation location. Records for so-called course shelf items, photocopied excerpts from books and journals and most of the e-reserve materials, in most cases differed so dramatically from their full bibliographic parents that the only field retained was a title field. In a dumb-terminal world, the time saved by not having to retype a title may have been significant, but in a copy-and-paste world of computer mice it was less so. Despite partial awareness of its limitations, NOTIS reserve data was migrated, more to preserve the historical record of faculty use and copyright requests than to accommodate significant reuse of old data.

The most notable change from NOTIS to Voyager for reserve staff was the ability to provide clickable URLs in the public OPAC. This one improvement made the integration of print and electronic reserve lists worthwhile. The other features of Voyager reserve made the integration manageable. Key among these features was modular list management. Now, at last, items, lists of items, courses, professors, departments, and academic periods could all be managed independently (see fig. 3).

FIGURE 3   Linking a reserve list to a course in Voyager 99.1.1

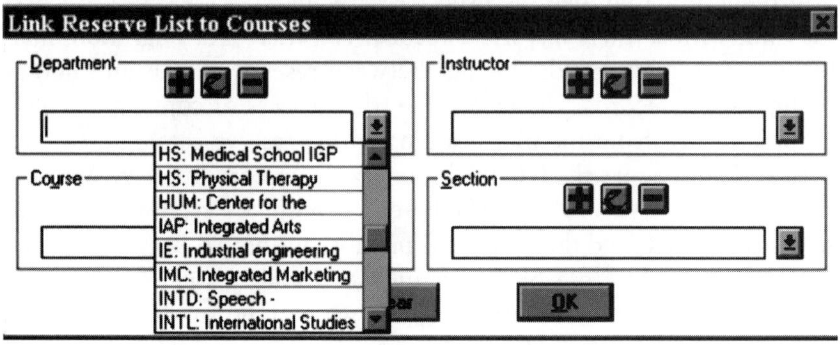

A list created for Professor Y's C05 class in spring 1999 can be easily reused for Professor Y's C20 class in fall 2000. When Northwestern first migrated to Voyager in fall 1998, the version then being used, 97.2, restricted the number of reserve lists to an arbitrary number based on the amount of total space left to hold the list title data in the underlying database tables. Since all reserve units are forced to share from the same pool of lists, care had to be taken to name them efficiently and not squander the available space. Thankfully, Voyager removed this limitation in the next release, and reserve units are now free to name lists as they choose. Items can be copied from list to list with relative ease, though each item must be made active individually once the piece has been physically processed or scanned (see fig. 4).

Removing items from lists is likewise a tedious, one-by-one process. An oddity of the Voyager system is that items which appear on two separate lists for the same professor will display twice in the OPAC even if only one list is active at any given time. A full explanation of this phenomenon has not yet been given.

FIGURE 4   Maintaining a reserve list in Voyager 99.1.1

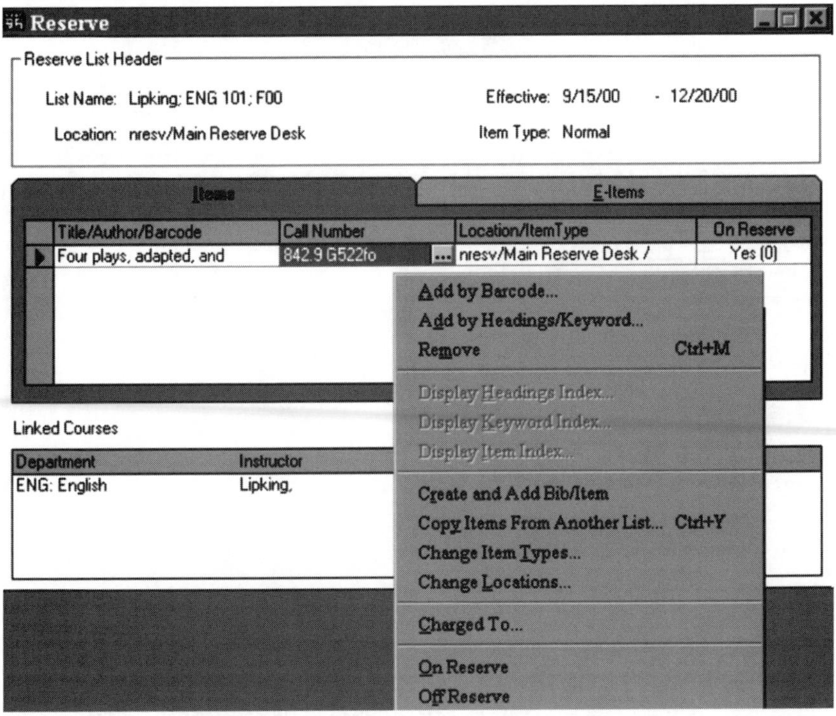

As a result of the Voyager implementation and integration of print and electronic reserves, a single search in the OPAC retrieves both types of documents. Search is performed by way of drop-down lists to combine professor, department, course, or section. All available items are displayed in a unified list regardless of format (see figs. 5 and 6).

PROBLEMS SOLVED, PROBLEMS CREATED, AND PROBLEMS THAT PERSIST

Switching to Voyager from NOTIS and static web pages solved many problems for the e-reserve processing operation. Efficiencies inherent in the Voyager software, including the more modular management of lists, save considerable processing time. The migration to Voyager did, however,

FIGURE 5   Voyager 99.1.1 course reserve search interface

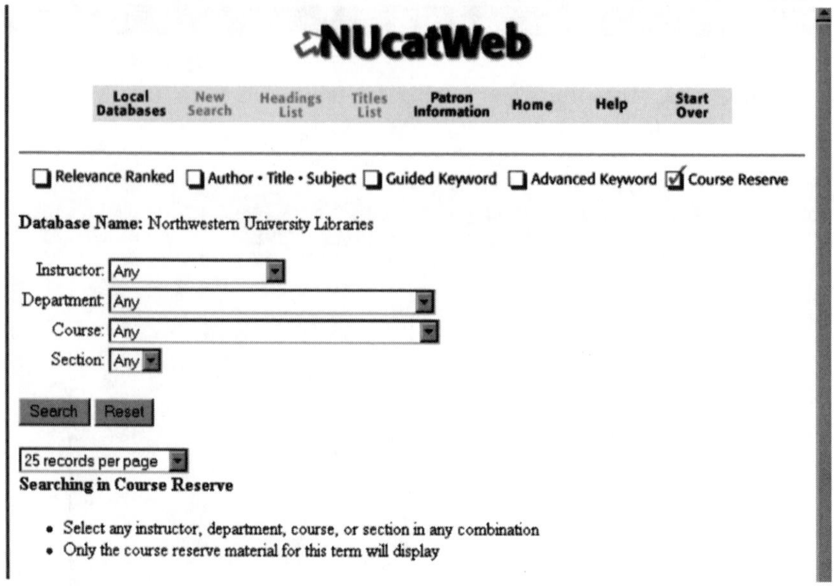

FIGURE 6A   Voyager 99.1.1 course reserve search results

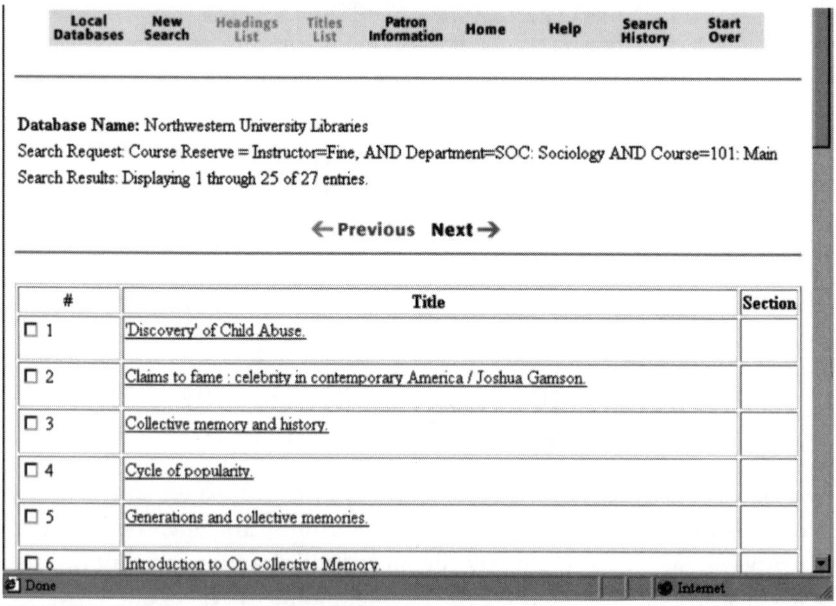

FIGURE 6B   Voyager 99.1.1 course reserve search results

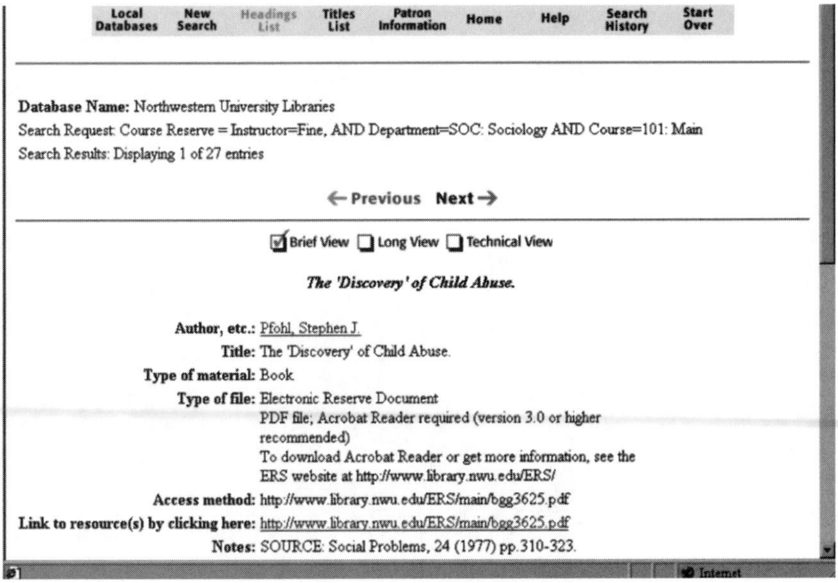

introduce new wrinkles and problems. Access to bibliographic records from the Voyager circulation client is severely restricted (see fig. 7).

In order to place access notes in the 516 field and add URLs to the 856 field, processing staff are forced to use the Voyager catalog client. Thankfully, Voyager has standardized the search options in staff mode across all of its clients, so the learning curve isn't excessively steep. Still, staff members are forced to switch between the circulation and catalog clients to complete records for e-reserve items.

Another problem created by the migration to Voyager is clutter in the main catalog. Records for items on reserve are marked "OPAC suppressed," which means that users will not retrieve reserve items when doing title searches in the OPAC. This does not, however, prevent staff from searching in the catalog or circulation clients from finding e-reserve and course shelf bibliographic and item records. Catalogers and other technical services staff must wade through the abbreviated reserve records to find bibliographic records for other library materials. At present, there is no function to exclude a specific location during a search, though it is possible to limit searches to a specific location or

FIGURE 7   Bib, holdings, and item view from Voyager 99.1.1 circulation module

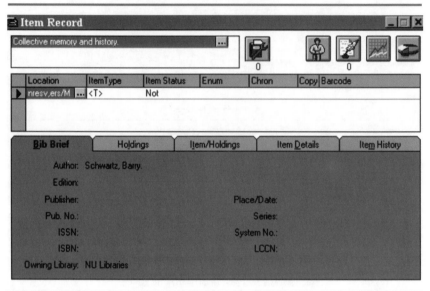

group of locations. This puts the burden on non-reserve staff to be on the lookout for reserve records.

Several problems present from the beginning of e-reserve at Northwestern remain. Key among these is the lack of appropriate access restriction measures. Although all items made available electronically are still IP-restricted, no further protections have been implemented. A year after Northwestern migrated to the Voyager system, the entire university migrated its registration and student systems to the PeopleSoft Student Enterprise system. This has led to unprecedented unification of authentication systems to give students a single point of access to their academic information but has not penetrated entirely to the library systems. Though the library receives some patron update information from the student systems, it still relies on the bar codes on Northwestern ID cards, or WildCards, as they are known, to uniquely identify users for all library system functions. Patron records in Voyager are therefore separated by a wide technical gap from course registration information in the university system. In addition, there are currently no mechanisms in the Voyager reserve system, or anywhere in the Voyager system, for that matter, to restrict access to particular library records or materials. Any protections must be put into place outside Voyager. Until a scalable technical solution can be found, e-reserves at Northwestern will continue with the protections it currently has.

It is still difficult to gather meaningful statistics on reserves from the Voyager system. Circulation statistics are not terribly useful since e-reserves do not technically circulate. Canned reports can show at any given time the status of expired, overdue, and circulating items for each list, but no summary of all lists or all items processed is yet available. Reserve statistics for the year following migration to Voyager are unavailable; now that higher-priority items have been dealt with, systems staff will be able to help generate customized reserve statistics.

Another problem not solved by migration to Voyager is one of faculty education and awareness of copyright restrictions. Specifically, making items accessible through Voyager does not discourage faculty from downloading individual e-reserve documents via 856 links and uploading them to their own course sites. This creates a potentially dangerous situation for the faculty member and the university because some faculty course sites are unrestricted and open to the world. The university's recent purchase of a Blackboard CourseInfo course management system may help curtail this behavior somewhat. CourseInfo will be discussed in some detail below.

Despite greatly streamlined management tools, another problem not yet solved with e-reserves is faculty request management. Since processing for print and electronic reserves progresses at a different pace, reserve staff have been using separate print forms to receive and track lists from faculty. These forms may be obtained on paper from the reserve staff or downloaded in PDF format from the Web. Because e-reserve scanning can take some time, staff request that faculty specify dates by which each piece is needed. During periods of high volume, work is prioritized and spaced out as necessary. This "just-in-time," calendar-based system is not managed electronically. With improvements to equipment and software in the area, the just-in-time approach is becoming less and less necessary, but highlights the fact that systems are always dependent on humans. Efficiency is greatly affected by faculty list submission preferences and the speed with which humans can process each piece. The Oracle database underlying the Voyager library system is complex enough that attempts to find a reasonable way to automate record creation directly from faculty requests have come so far to naught.

Purchase of a Blackboard CourseInfo course management system
has dramatically changed the way faculty and the university as a whole
think about providing electronic access to primary course material.
Until CourseInfo, ERS was the only large-scale service for managing
and delivering electronic course material to Northwestern students. The
process of finding space on a web server, learning to use a web author-
ing tool, and designing a navigable, maintainable site was enough of a
barrier to prevent most faculty members from even attempting it. They
contented themselves with providing reading materials within the
restrictions imposed by the ERS system and staff.

Now, however, all faculty need to understand is how to operate a
web browser in order to create a web space for each of their courses,
managing and maintaining their own document stores. However, faculty must still depend on reserve staff for the significant document conversion, copyright clearance, and content organization services provided through ERS. Therefore, better methods for making links
between ERS and CourseInfo must be found.

Late in the academic year 1999, library staff developed a method of
permanently bookmarking searches in the library catalog. Previously,
the Voyager system environment used session variables encoded within
the URL string to render bookmarks useless once the session timed out.
Now that this bookmarking scheme, the NUcat Persistent URL (or simply NUcat PURL), has been developed, faculty may make links into
their Voyager reserve lists from anywhere else on the Web, including
from within CourseInfo web sites.[3] Improving on such opportunities
for linkage is a challenge staff in reserve units will undertake in the
coming year. Collaboration between library and information technology staff has never been more critical.

CONVERSION CONSIDERATIONS

What are some key questions to ask when converting to IOLS-based
management of e-reserves?

- What kind of hyperlinking and document management do you
  need? What does the system support? This is important not only
  for e-reserve services. As digital library initiatives grow, more
  libraries may find themselves organizing digital files of all kinds:
  individual image files, PDF documents, sound and image files,

HTML, XML, and SGML files. Coming up with meaningful naming schemes and directory structures can be a headache. Look for a library system that may be able to manage some of these things for you. Be sure your system can support all of the document types you wish to deliver or link to for e-reserves.

- Will integrating print and e-reserves save or create work for the staff? Are these beasts at all similar? Do faculty request that both print and electronic materials be made available for a single course? Even with different materials in different formats, a volume operation might realize significant time savings by using a single system for managing both kinds of reserve items in a single list.

- What kinds of copyright management tools are there? This is very important. Most libraries will want their library system to help them track when requests must be made or royalties paid.

- Can the library system receive reserve pick lists or requests directly from the faculty member? This can greatly speed record creation and item retrieval because it can be tied to items known to exist in the library catalog.

- Can the library system be extended to integrate with existing campus authentication schemes? Is it possible to group users by course registration and put access restrictions in place?

- What kind of statistics will you be able to extract from the system? If you must track print and electronic materials separately, be sure there is a mechanism in the IOLS to identify each.

Compose a wish list for a library system's reserve functions and make sure they're included in any RFPs or RFIs. Some excellent recent examples of RFPs that address the e-reserve issue are available on the Web. Of particular interest are the University of Iowa's RFP, Minnesota Library Information Network's RFP, and Harvard University's functional checklist for reserve. All three of these documents are linked from the Florida Center for Library Automation's LMS Committee home page.[4] Also worth visiting is the Integrated Library System Reports site, which has links to sample RFPs and to IOLS vendor pages as well as the results of its 1999 vendor survey.[5]

Northwestern's experience has shown that, apart from the paramount need for active links to digital documents, some of the most important library system considerations for reserves and e-reserves are not specific to the final formats of the material. They more often pertain to request and workflow management, bibliographic control, and a meaningful public search interface to allow students to locate materials by course or professor. Homegrown systems are, by definition, a closer match for some specific e-reserve functions. However, Northwestern found that the time saved by maintaining a single system was worth some trade-offs in flexibility and that the added convenience for users was considerable.

NOTES

1. Kevin Hughes developed the original SWISH or Simple Web Indexing System for Humans; this product is currently supported as SWISH-E by staff at the University of California, at sunsite.berkeley.edu/SWISH-E.
2. CONFU report. CONFU never approved the guidelines for electronic reserves, so they are not part of the official text of the report, which is available from the U.S. Patent and Trademark Office's web site: www.uspto.gov/web/offices/dcom/olia/confu. However, they are available on a number of web sites, including the excellent UT System's Crash Course on Copyright, at www.utsystem.edu/OGC/IntellectualProperty/rsrvguid.htm.
3. NUcat is the name of the Northwestern University catalog. The library is phasing out references to the Voyager system in favor of NUcat.
4. Florida Center for Library Automation's LMS Committee home page: fcla.edu/FCLAinfo/lms/lmspg.html.
5. Integrated Library System Reports (ILSR): www.ilsr.com.

5

ONCORES
A Homegrown E-Reserve System

WAYNE R. PERRYMAN

T his chapter details the local development of ONCORES, the web-based electronic reserve system in use at the Humboldt State University Library. Humboldt State is the northernmost of the twenty-three campuses in the California State University (CSU) system and was one of the first sites within that system to adopt an active electronic reserve system. The ensuing discussion explores the campus environment, the issues and considerations that were addressed during the development of the ONCORES system, and future trends in electronic reserves at Humboldt.

BACKGROUND

Humboldt State is located on the remote north coast of California, flanked by the Pacific Ocean on one side and the Coast Range on the other. Nestled among the coast redwoods, the region has traditionally been dependent upon the lumber industry and tourism for its economic base. The Humboldt region is imbued with a rich Native American heritage as well as an appreciation for the arts, with the campus serving as a catalyst for cultural offerings in the area.

Humboldt State has an enrollment of approximately 7,500 students taught by more than 400 faculty. The university has well-regarded programs in the arts, humanities, social sciences, and environmental and natural sciences. It is consistently ranked in the top 10 percent of all United States universities and colleges in terms of academic quality.

The university is a four-hour drive from the closest metropolitan area and any sister campuses. Given its isolated locale, campus leaders have long been interested in harnessing new technologies to serve the needs of its students and faculty. Distance education and remote access have become buzzwords in recent years, as the campus has worked to grow its technological base. These efforts have been spurred on by the rapid expansion of the World Wide Web and the promulgation of a more robust telecommunications infrastructure, which have, in turn, helped to offset the limitations brought about by the physical isolation of the campus. It is within this environmental context that the ON-CORES system was conceived and developed.

INITIAL STEPS:
DEVELOPMENT OF THE ONCORES MODEL

The development of the ONCORES system began in earnest with the creation of the access services department in the Humboldt State University Library in July 1995. That department consisted of the acquisitions, cataloging, circulation, periodicals, and systems units, with activities centered around the Geac ADVANCE integrated library system. The chair of that department undertook an initial exploration of the issues entailed in creating an electronic reserve system. Following that review, a team was created to undertake a more thorough investigation and develop a pilot program. The initial process carried out by this team included:

- a review of the extant professional literature
- a survey of the marketplace to identify applicable software and hardware
- a review of electronic reserve models used by other academic libraries
- an analysis of local campus course reserve needs
- consideration of copyright issues
- a review of staffing and budgetary requirements
- initiation of an electronic reserve pilot project

The remainder of this section discusses each of these steps in more detail.

A Review of the Extant Professional Literature

When the Humboldt team began its investigation in late 1995, the literature on electronic reserves was scant. In fact, very few libraries were actually serving reserve readings electronically at that time, although many were considering the possibility and exploring the issues. However, several important articles and other publications were issued in the early to mid-1990s, which did help to inform the developmental process at Humboldt. Those publications are listed at the end of this chapter.

A Survey of the Marketplace to Identify Applicable Software and Hardware

Team members explored various software and hardware options that might be applicable to the reserve operation at Humboldt. In particular, the team focused upon the scanning and imaging technology that was available at that time and the hardware needed to use it. Their survey included discussions with software vendors, librarians, and others familiar with the application of such software in a library setting. The team got hands-on experience with several software packages, including Adobe Acrobat Pro for portable document format (PDF) and Xerox Textbridge Pro and Caere OmniPage Pro for the optical character recognition (OCR) format. The team also explored the use of Photoshop as a possible tool for helping prepare image files for electronic delivery.

The team also needed to give serious thought to the operating system because the library was in a state of transition. When the electronic reserve concept was initially envisioned, the library was using a combination of Windows 3.1 and Novell NetWare for its local area network architecture. With the release of the Windows 95 operating system in August 1995, however, there was serious discussion of consolidating the operating system under the Windows umbrella.

The hardware review included consideration of the personal computer configuration for the staff machines that would be required to convert and prepare the electronic documents for delivery, including scanners, printers, and other peripherals; the servers and storage media needed to serve and store the necessary files; and the level of personal computer the public would need to access and use the online documents. The team needed to plan for the hardware infrastructure to be scalable so that it could expand over time along with the anticipated growth in demand for electronic reserve services.

Team members reviewed a number of commercial electronic reserve systems that were developing during this time, including the Contec Data Systems C3 Electronic Course Reserves module, the Docutek ERes system, and the Nousoft ECR software. Although it would not be available until 1997, they also monitored the development of the Geac ADVANCE online public access catalog (OPAC) web interface, GeoWeb, to determine if it might eventually provide a mechanism for organizing and serving electronic reserve documents.

A Review of Electronic Reserve Models
Used by Other Academic Libraries

As noted, relatively few academic libraries were actively serving reserve readings electronically during the initial phases of the Humboldt investigation. Among those libraries that were providing such a service at that time, the Humboldt team identified two predominant models. One model used the Web for both in-house and remote delivery, while the other used proprietary software, either developed locally or purchased from a software vendor, to provide in-library access via dedicated terminals or personal computers.

An Analysis of Local Course Reserve Needs

Although the Web had become a significant information access and delivery tool in 1994, Humboldt State University did not begin to develop a serious web presence until 1996. The library did, however, have one of the first departmental home pages on campus, beginning with a prototype that was brought up in the spring of 1995. Over ensuing months, the library staff began to use that site to draw together disparate electronic resources and to provide information about library programs and services.

Through discussions with faculty members who were using the print reserve services, the library was able to determine that there would be a market for an electronic reserve program. The primary question was how best to configure such a program to serve the needs and requirements of the Humboldt community. That question would need to be addressed during a forthcoming pilot project.

Consideration of Copyright Issues

Copyright issues are important concerns in developing an electronic reserve program or, for that matter, any program that seeks to redistribute copyright-protected materials electronically. An institution's interpretation of copyright law could be the deciding factor in determining whether an electronic reserve system will prove viable at that particular site. This interpretation will guide the selection of materials to be placed on reserve and will determine what role, if any, copyright clearance will play in the service.

In its review of copyright considerations, the Humboldt team sought guidance from a variety of sources, including the California State University System, the Association of Research Libraries, and copyright experts in the field. Team members attended copyright workshops on campus and at conferences, researched the literature, consulted copyright web sites, and participated in electronic discussion lists of related issues.

As a member of the CSU system, Humboldt was especially interested in any guidance that the system might provide in this regard. Although the CSU system did not offer direct, definitive guidelines addressing copyright in the electronic arena, it did, in cooperation with the State University of New York and the City College of New York, issue four booklets addressing copyright and related issues. The series was issued under the aegis of the Consortium for Educational Technology for University Systems (CETUS) in 1997 and has been a valuable point of reference in addressing such questions. Finally, the Humboldt State University campus issued a copying policy in 1990 that extended to both print and electronic resources.

Based upon its review of the research available at that time and consultation with experts in the field, the team concluded that the library could, under the provisions of the United States Code, title 17, section 107: Limitations on Exclusive Rights: Fair Use, serve copyright-protected reserve materials electronically. The key issues the library would have to heed were embodied in the following quote from section 107:

In determining whether the use made of a work in any particular case is a fair use the factors to be considered shall include—

1. the purpose and character of the use, including whether such use is of a commercial nature or is for nonprofit educational purposes;
2. the nature of the copyrighted work;
3. the amount and substantiality of the portion used in relation to the copyrighted work as a whole; and
4. the effect of the use upon the potential market for or value of the copyrighted work.

In order to protect the interests and rights of copyright holders while at the same time serving the needs of its users, the library would need to include certain safeguards when providing electronic access to copyright-protected resources. Those safeguards would be based upon an analysis of the four factors of fair use as they relate to each category of reserve material requested by a faculty member.

A Review of Staffing and Budgetary Requirements

At the time this investigation was under way, the library had not earmarked any additional funds for the creation of an electronic reserve service. It was assumed, of course, that additional hardware and software would be required to develop and implement such a program and that a proposal outlining these needs would be written at a later date.

The initial assumption regarding staffing was that the electronic reserve service could be rolled into existing reserve operations, which consisted of one full-time library assistant working with a cadre of student assistants. It was felt that electronic reserves would replace print reserves on a quid pro quo basis—an assumption that was not supported by subsequent experience.

Initiation of Electronic Reserve Pilot Project

By late 1995, the library planning team felt it had enough information to move ahead with a pilot project and gain some practical hands-on experience. During its initial investigation, the team had determined that, based upon the personnel, budget, and technology available at the time, the library should explore the possibility of using the Web to serve reserve readings electronically in Adobe Acrobat PDF format. Purchase of one of the off-the-shelf commercial electronic reserve systems available at that time, such as Contec C3 or Nousoft, was out of the question from a budgetary standpoint. Those systems also included features, such as copyright tracking and compliance modules, that would not be particularly useful in the Humboldt environment, since the library had decided to exercise its fair-use privileges and not request copyright permissions. The investigative team also wanted to explore the use of the Web to provide broad remote access to reserve readings. Remote access would not be possible using a system of dedicated terminals available in-house, as some libraries had developed or adopted before the advent of the Web.

THE ELECTRONIC RESERVES PILOT PROJECT

It was with these goals in mind that in December 1995 the chair of the access services department submitted a proposal to the library administration to create an electronic reserve system development team. That team, consisting of the department chair (who would also serve as chair of the project team), the head of the circulation unit, the head of the systems unit, and the reserves coordinator, would be charged with developing and executing an electronic reserve pilot project. That pilot was to be carried out within the circulation unit, which already managed the print reserves.

Specifically, the proposal called for the team to:

recruit up to five faculty members, representing all four colleges of the university, who would be willing to participate in the development and testing of a possible electronic reserves model;

carry out the project during the spring 1996 semester, running from January 22 through May 22;

brief faculty participants on the project scope, parameters, and objectives, including discussion of project timelines, how to contribute to and access electronic reserve documents, copyright issues, etc.;

create a separate file and directory structure for each course on the library web server;

build an electronic reserves web site that would be accessible via the library home page, with information and instructions for student and faculty participants;

scan and convert submitted hardcopy materials to the Adobe Acrobat PDF;

address copyright compliance issues, following current fair-use guidelines;

establish a computer workstation in the reserves unit replete with the hardware and software needed for scanning and manipulating images, creating and updating files, communicating with the participating faculty and students via e-mail, etc.;

explore whether image files should be stored and served from a library computer or from a remote web server managed by the campus computing and telecommunications services division;

evaluate the impact of the new service upon the existing reserve operation, with particular focus on staffing workloads, levels, and responsibilities;

draft policies and procedures to integrate electronic and print reserve operations;

identify and address the training needs of the students, faculty, and staff working on the project;

determine how best to communicate with electronic reserve users and publicize the service to the campus community;

evaluate the results of the pilot project, soliciting feedback from the project participants, directly observing program utilization, and analyzing appropriate statistical measures;

make a recommendation to the library administration at the end of the pilot project as to the long-term viability of the locally developed electronic reserves model.

The administration approved the pilot proposal later in December 1995.

LESSONS LEARNED:
PILOT PROJECT ANALYSIS AND RETOOLING

As soon as the team received administrative approval for the pilot project, it began to put together the necessary components. This process took longer than originally anticipated, however, and the infrastructure was not yet in place as the spring semester began on January 22.

Through the hard work of the library team members, the team leader was able to formally initiate the project on February 22 with a meeting of the project team and five faculty participants whom he had recruited. At that meeting he briefed the attendees on the project goals, objectives, and issues; reviewed copyright and fair-use policy issues; outlined the scope of the pilot project; described how to access and use the electronic reserve documents; and demonstrated the fledgling electronic reserve system.

During the remainder of the spring 1996 semester, the team successfully fulfilled the project objectives, establishing the hardware/software infrastructure to support the electronic reserves pilot, building a prototype website, drafting supporting documentation, and working closely with the faculty participants to evaluate the outcomes of the project. During that first semester, the library created twenty-five PDF documents in support of seven classes. Those documents were accessed 578 times, representing approximately 4 percent of reserve usage during that time period.

Copyright Compliance
in the Electronic Reserve Environment

As previously noted, the library's intent was to exercise its right of fair use in providing access to copyright-protected works through the electronic reserve system. Part of that process was to involve an evaluation of each course reserve request on the basis of the four factors of fair use outlined in section 107 of the Copyright Act. Another key component was to be the application of the Humboldt State University copying policy, dated June 4, 1990, to the online environment (see appendix I).

The electronic reserves file structure and services were designed to promote copyright compliance. In order to ensure that the rights of all would be protected, the team decided to embed the following four elements in every copyright-protected work served through the electronic reserve system:

1. a statement warning of copyright restrictions
2. password protection restricting electronic reserve file access to students enrolled in participating classes
3. hierarchical access by department/course/instructor, rather than by a document's author or title

4. full bibliographic attribution, including author, title, date, source, page numbers, etc.

Resources Served through the Electronic Reserve System

Early on in the pilot project, the library development team determined that it could serve a full range of documents through the electronic reserve system, including those protected by copyright, as long as it heeded the established policies related to fair use. Resources that were to be served through the system included:

- journal articles
- book chapters
- course syllabi
- course reading lists
- lecture notes
- examinations
- problem sets
- links to copyright-free or copyright-compliant web sites

Pilot Project: Phase II

Despite the overall success of the pilot following its initial launch, the project team felt that it had not had enough practical experience to move the service into production. A number of pivotal questions remained to be addressed, including:

- staffing
- image quality
- access to the image files
- evolving copyright and fair-use policies in the electronic realm
- the interaction of electronic reserves services with other campus computing services and facilities

In August 1996, the team recommended and received administrative approval to continue the pilot project for the 1996–1997 academic year. During that year, the team would recruit several additional faculty participants and tackle the outstanding issues, while continuing to test and evaluate the existing model using PDF images to serve electronic documents over the Web.

For the fall 1996 semester, the team successfully expanded the number of faculty working on the project from five to eight, in the process replacing a few of the original participants who were no longer available. It worked closely with those faculty members to evaluate the success of the current model. Over the course of that semester, the team would identify several issues that would ultimately raise serious doubts about the viability of the PDF-based model in the current campus environment.

In a mid-year report to faculty participants in January 1997, the team leader summarized the shortcomings that the project members had identified during the previous semester. He also addressed several modifications to the project model that the library team was exploring to remedy those shortcomings.

While emphasizing that the electronic reserve system was still very much under development, as practical and technological issues remained to be addressed, the team leader's report noted some specific problems that related directly to the use of PDF documents and the limitations of the Adobe Acrobat 2.0 software. To wit:

Large online document files with excessive download times. This issue was especially problematic for remote users who were attempting to access the reserve readings via a modem, which, at the time, had a maximum transfer rate of 28.8 kilobytes per second (kps).

Poor on-screen readability. While the PDF software retained the image of the original document, the user was often forced to magnify the image substantially in order to be able to read it online. On the positive side, it was possible to produce an excellent printed document from the Acrobat Reader, regardless of the onscreen legibility.

Limited access to the Adobe Acrobat Reader software in the campus computing labs. In order to use the PDF files, the client workstation required the installation of the Adobe Acrobat Reader. At the time the pilot project was under way, the Reader was not yet included in the standard workstation configuration in the campus computing labs.

In addition to the problems related to the use of PDF files, the report also noted the need for additional end-user information/documentation about the electronic reserves program.

PDF versus HTML:
A Practical Comparison

As soon as it became apparent during the fall 1996 semester that there were problems related to the use of PDF files, the team began to explore other delivery options. Since the library was determined to use the World Wide Web to provide access to electronic reserve materials, an obvious alternative to PDF was HTML (hypertext markup language), the native source code of the Web. The team undertook a comparison of PDF and optical character recognition-to-HTML software packages, identifying the advantages and disadvantages of each approach based upon the capabilities of the hardware and software available at that time. The results of this comparison can be summarized as follows:

Portable Document Format

Advantages

Scanning directly to PDF provides an accurate representation of the original document including text and graphics, especially when printed on a quality printer.

Scanning directly to PDF is fast and requires less staff time than other methods.

Disadvantages

User-installed external viewing software (Acrobat Reader) is required to view the PDF documents.

Scanning creates large files, making remote access via a modem extremely slow.

On-screen readability of PDF documents is poor.

PDF documents require a relatively large amount of disk storage space.

Users cannot search within a PDF document.

PDF documents cannot be e-mailed to most university computers due to campus quota limitations.

PDF documents cannot be displayed using the Lynx text-mode web browser.

OCR/HTML

Advantages

Graphical web browsers can display the document without special viewing software.

HTML documents consume relatively little disk storage space.

Given smaller file sizes and the use of native HTML, remote users could access the documents via modem.

On-screen readability of HTML documents is very good.

Users can search from within an HTML document.

Depending upon the graphic content of the pages, most HTML documents can be e-mailed to other campus computers.

HTML documents can be displayed using the Lynx text-mode web browser, except for graphic content.

Disadvantages

Due to the vagaries of the OCR conversion process and the inherent limitations of the software, errors will be introduced into the converted document.

Additional staff time would be required to proofread documents, correct errors, create special files for graphics and non-Roman characters, etc.

Overall staff time required to process a document for electronic reserves would increase.

The converted HTML document would not have the same page layout and fonts as the original.

Electronic Reserves Moves to HTML

Given its experiences in the fall of 1996 and its analysis of the pros and cons of using PDF compared with HTML, the library project team decided to adopt a delivery model based predominantly on OCR/HTML for the duration of the pilot project. Since it would continue using PDF for certain types of documents that would not convert well to HTML, the team also decided to upgrade its Acrobat software from version 2.0 to 3.0. The team leader met several times with the head of the academic computing department and was successful in having Acrobat Reader added to the standard software configuration for university computing labs. The Reader software was also added to the configuration for all web-accessible personal computers within the library facility itself.

Anticipating that the creation of HTML documents would be more time-consuming and might require additional staffing resources, in March 1997 the library purchased a second high-end workstation, a higher quality scanner, and supporting software dedicated to the electronic reserve operation. Additional web-capable machines that could be used to access electronic reserve readings from within the building were added in the public area of the library. Finally, the team leader redoubled his efforts to update and create instructional aids for electronic reserves and to provide information to current and potential users of the service. Most of that information was to be made accessible via the electronic reserve web site.

The pilot project drew to a successful conclusion at the end of the spring 1997 semester, using the bifurcated model of serving a combination of HTML and PDF documents. Over the following summer, team members made the necessary preparations to move from pilot to production at the beginning of the fall 1997 semester.

ONCORES TAKES OFF:
BEYOND THE PILOT AND INTO PRODUCTION

The ONCORES Web Site

In August 1997, the electronic reserve system was officially introduced as a new library service. Over that summer, the team leader completed the various components of the electronic reserve web site. The site presently includes informational pages targeted to students and faculty, respectively. To assist in marketing and name recognition for its new service, the library adopted the name ONCORES, or Online Course Reserve System.

The primary gateway into ONCORES is its main menu (appendix II). From that gateway, students and faculty may access resources targeted to their needs.

For students, the ONCORES site includes:

- a password-protected link to the ONCORES readings (appendix III)
- a brief guide to the ONCORES service (appendix IV)
- a single-screen quick guide to accessing ONCORES (appendix V)

ONCORES links for faculty include:

- information about the ONCORES service (appendix VI)
- an ONCORES page with frequently asked questions (appendix VII)
- an online ONCORES reserve request form (appendix VIII)
- a brief PowerPoint slide show about ONCORES

Marketing the New Service

The library has used a variety of techniques to market the ONCORES service, such as:

- adoption of the catchy ONCORES name
- a prominent link on the HSU Library home page
- targeted user information at the ONCORES web site
- presentation at annual faculty reception hosted by library
- faculty orientation seminars
- bulk e-mail messages to faculty
- feature articles in the *Lumberjack* campus newspaper
- informational handouts at the reserve desk
- interview on the campus radio station
- word-of-mouth testimonials from satisfied customers

All communications regarding ONCORES highlighted the system's services, design elements, and benefits, including:

- convenience
- ease of use
- single point of entry for reserve readings
- web accessibility on and off campus
- unlimited simultaneous use—readings never "checked out"
- 24/7 availability
- copyright compliance

Staffing Issues in the Production Environment

Staffing remains a key issue in the development and expansion of the ONCORES service. No additional permanent staff have been added to the circulation operation since the advent of the pilot program. Rather, some staff responsibilities within the circulation unit have been reassigned so that a library assistant could be dedicated to the ONCORES service on a full-time basis. However, additional student assistant support has been required in order for ONCORES to meet its production targets.

One of the early assumptions of the development team—that the advent of an electronic reserve system would lead to a concomitant decrease in the use of the print reserve services—has not materialized, at least not yet. Both print and electronic reserve services continue to be in demand, although, as might be expected, ONCORES is showing the most growth. As long as this trend continues, the library will need to monitor staffing needs within the reserve operation and add personnel as required to support the demand for these important services.

ONCORES Production Statistics, 1998–2000

As noted, ONCORES has been well received by the faculty and students at Humboldt State. In fact, the demand for ONCORES services has increased steadily during each semester since the system went into development. It is germane to put ONCORES into the context of the overall course reserves operation, to reflect the proportion of that operation which it represents and to give some indication of its potential for future expansion.

Over the past four semesters, encompassing the 1998–1999 and 1999–2000 academic years, the library reserve service has accumulated the following statistics:

Statistical Category	*ONCORES*	*Print*	*Totals*
Number of Items Served	1,230 (19%)	5,343 (81%)	6,573
Number of Participating Instructors	129 (14%)	816 (86%)	945
Number of Courses Served	168 (8%)	2,036 (92%)	2,204
Number of Uses ("hits" or checkouts)	40,832 (31%)	89,605 (69%)	130,437

These statistics reveal some trends with respect to reserve services:

> Overall, course reserves continues to be a heavily used library service.
>
> ONCORES represents a relatively small proportion of overall reserve activities.
>
> Readership rates are disproportionately higher for ONCORES than for print reserve materials.

CURRENT DEVELOPMENTS, FUTURE TRENDS

ONCORES could potentially fall prey to its own success. As the cumulative statistics covering the past four semesters indicate, ONCORES has been a popular service among the campus community. And yet, despite showing steady growth since its introduction, ONCORES still represents a relatively small proportion of reserve activity when compared with print reserve statistics for the same time period. Clearly, there is much growth potential in the use of ONCORES, particularly as the university and library continue their migration to an electronic delivery model for many academic support services. At the same time, it is unlikely that ONCORES will be able to garner additional personnel resources to meet increases in demand, unless those resources are redirected from other services. Consequently, the library must do whatever it can to maximize its available staffing resources. To that end, several options are presently under serious consideration or development by the library ONCORES team.

Is a Return to PDF in the Future of ONCORES?

The answer to this question is a resounding yes—especially since the library needs to continue expanding ONCORES services without adding personnel. The current quest to maximize efficiency has included a reassessment of the use of PDF to serve the online documents. From the time ONCORES went into production in the fall of 1997 through the spring of 2000, virtually all online articles were provided in HTML format. As noted earlier, HTML does offer a number of access and display advantages for the end user in the web environment. However, these advantages come at a cost to the library in terms of the substantial staff time required to convert, proofread, and serve the online HTML documents.

In an effort to boost ONCORES production and serve more classes without adding staff, the library decided to reincorporate PDF into its processing model, beginning with the fall 2000 semester. The library anticipates that it will serve approximately two-thirds of ONCORES documents in that format, with the remainder continuing to be primarily in HTML.

Several of the issues the electronic reserve development team encountered during its initial examination of the Adobe Acrobat PDF software have since been addressed. For example, the current version of Acrobat software, coupled with Acrobat Reader 4.0, allows the user to begin reading a document as soon as the first page is available, rather than having to wait for the entire file to finish downloading, as in earlier versions of the software. Also, modem transfer rates have increased from 28.8kps to 56kps or more, greatly increasing the speed at which home users may download the files. Likewise, the use of the Acrobat Reader has become far more pervasive in the educational, business, and home computing environments over the past several years, particularly as electronic content providers have adopted it as a standard delivery format.

What Role Might Aggregator Services Play in ONCORES?

Another efficiency measure being explored by the ONCORES team is the use of full-text documents that are already available electronically in one or more of the numerous aggregator services to which the library subscribes. The library provides its users with access to an increasing array of online full-text services, including EBSCOHost Academic Search Elite, EBSCO Online, Lexis-Nexis, ABI/Inform, Omnifile Full Text Mega, CINAHL, Dow Jones Interactive, JSTOR, E*Subscribe, Wiley Interscience, and ProQuest Newstand, among others. Humboldt also subscribes to a custom search interface that was developed by the staff of the Meriam Library at CSU-Chico. That interface enables a library user or staff member to simultaneously search for a journal title across many of these full-text databases. This year, ONCORES staff plan to incorporate such a search into their processing workflow, in hopes of finding articles requested by the faculty in electronic format, which they can then link from within the ONCORES search directory. It remains to be seen what percentage of requested articles will be found in a full-text database, but this number can only be expected to increase as the aggregators work to increase the breadth and depth of their online offerings.

What Is the Relationship between ONCORES and the OPAC?

To date, the ONCORES service has been provided via the Web, entirely independent of the library online public access catalog. In 1999, however, Humboldt State implemented a web-based Endeavor Voyager OPAC, which raises the possibility that ONCORES readings might be served from both within and outside the OPAC. In fact, beginning with the spring 2000 semester, print reserve titles have been included in the OPAC. Including ONCORES records, along with their direct password-protected links to the articles, would clearly be a benefit to the end user. However, this added service would again come at the expense of the finite staff time the library has available to process ONCORES materials and will have to be weighed accordingly.

Copyright, Copyright, Copyright, or
"Fair Use, Abuse, or No Use"

To date, the library has been confident that it can safely serve course reserve materials electronically under the fair-use provisions of the United States Code, title 17, section 107. At the same time, copyright issues in the electronic realm have been hotly debated in recent years, with no end in sight. Noteworthy examples include initiatives such as the moribund Conference on Fair Use (CONFU) and the *Fair Use Guidelines for Educational Multimedia* developed by the Consortium of College and University Media Centers.

There is also the risk that new legislation might impede the ability of libraries to continue serving these resources. Although it did not specifically abridge library rights, the Digital Millennium Copyright Act, which was signed into law on October 28, 1998, did serve notice to many in the field that major new copyright legislation was indeed possible. Librarians, educators, and civil libertarians from around the country must continue to monitor, direct, and participate in these discussions on an ongoing basis. We must contest any attempts to limit or otherwise abridge the right of libraries to continue to serve copyrighted materials in furtherance of the educational process, as originally envisioned in section 107.

What Other File Formats Should ONCORES Support?

Thus far, the vast majority of information resources placed on reserve through ONCORES have been journal articles. In some instances, particularly under the HTML service model, those articles have required the creation of a GIF or JPEG image file to display and link a graphic contained in the article, such as a chart, table, map, or picture. This need has diminished with the reintroduction of PDF as the primary file format, since PDF is generally able to accommodate graphics. ONCORES staff members have occasionally been asked to provide a link to a web site, but the preponderance of data served through ONCORES to date has been textual in nature.

Library planners have long been anticipating that, with the surge of interest in all things multimedia, particularly among the younger faculty and students, we would be asked to serve other formats through ONCORES, such as streaming audio or video. Although the library is prepared for this eventuality, the demand for such support has not yet materialized.

CONCLUSION

Using the experiences at Humboldt State University, this chapter has addressed the major issues any library must confront when developing its own electronic reserve service. Some of these issues can be addressed and resolved early in the process, while others, such as copyright, require ongoing vigilance and oversight. Of course, rapidly evolving technologies will likewise be a major determinant in future directions for such services. It is gratifying to note that, based upon the Humboldt experience, an electronic reserve service can be developed and supported alongside a more traditional print reserve model. Consequently, rather than simply replacing one service with the other, a balance must be struck between the two, taking many practical questions into account. This dichotomy will present many interesting challenges for a library as it determines how best to employ technology to serve the needs of its users.

For additional information, follow the ONCORES links on the Humboldt State University Library home page, library.humboldt.edu.

SELECTED REFERENCES

Bosseau, Don L. "Anatomy of a Small Step Forward: The Electronic Reserve Book Room at San Diego State University." *Journal of Academic Librarianship* 18, no. 6 (January 1993): 366–68.

Butler, Brett. "Electronic Course Reserves and Digital Libraries: Progenitor and Prognosis." *Journal of Academic Librarianship* 22, no. 2 (March 1996): 124–27.

CSU–SUNY–CUNY Joint Committee (under sponsorship of the Consortium for Educational Technology for University Systems). *The Academic Library in the Information Age: Changing Roles.* Seal Beach, Calif.: California State University, 1997.

———. *Fair Use of Copyrighted Works: A Crucial Element in Educating America.* Seal Beach, Calif.: California State University, 1997.

———. *Information Resources and Library Services for Distance Learners: A Framework for Quality.* Seal Beach, Calif.: California State University, 1997.

———. *Ownership of New Works at the University: Unbundling of Rights and the Pursuit of Higher Learning.* Seal Beach, Calif.: California State University, 1997.

Enssle, Halcyon R. "Reserve On-line: Bringing Reserve into the Electronic Age." *Information Technology and Libraries* 13, no. 3 (September 1994): 197–201.

Goodrum, Richard. "The E-RBR: Confirming the Technology and Exploring the Law of Electronic Reserves: Two Generations of the Digital Library System at the SDSU Library." *Journal of Academic Librarianship* 22, no. 2 (March 1996): 118–23.

Kesten, Philip R., and Slaven M. Zivkovic. "ERes—Electronic Resources on the World Wide Web." *Journal of Interlibrary Loan, Document Delivery & Information Supply* 7, no. 4 (1997): 37–47.

Kristof, Cindy. "Electronic Reserves Operations in ARL Libraries." SPEC Kit 245. Washington, D.C.: Association of Research Libraries, 1999.

Schmidt, Steven, and David Lewis. "The Unlimited Potential of the Electronic Library (Except Where Prohibited by the Copyright Law)." Paper presented at *Computers in Libraries '96*. Washington, D.C., February 27, 1996.

Seaman, Scott. "Copyright and Fair Use in an Electronic Reserves System." *Journal of Interlibrary Loan, Document Delivery & Information Supply* 7, no. 2 (1996): 19–28.

Soete, George J. "Transforming Libraries: Issues and Innovations in Electronic Reserves." SPEC Kit 217. Washington, D.C.: Association of Research Libraries, 1996.

APPENDIX I

Humboldt State University
Copying Policy

Office of the President
UNIVERSITY MANAGEMENT LETTER NO. 90-2
Copying Policy
June 4, 1990

It is University policy to adhere to the provisions of the Copyright Revision Act, Title 17 of the United States Code (Public Law 94-553). This policy, enumerated below, is based on the Guidelines for Classroom Copying in Not-for-Profit Educational Institutions, as published in the House Judiciary Committee Report on the Copyright Bill.

1. Allowable copying from copyrighted material.
    1.1   A single copy may be made of the following:
        1.1.1   A chapter from a book.
        1.1.2   An article from a periodical or newspaper.
        1.1.3   A short story, short essay or short poem.
        1.1.4   A chart, a graph, a diagram, a drawing, a cartoon, or a picture.

    1.2. Multiple copying for classroom use is permitted if the following conditions are met:
        1.2.1   Brevity
            a. A complete poem, if less than 250 words, or an excerpt of 250 words from a longer poem.
            b. A complete article, story, or essay, if less than 2,500 words, or not more than 1,000 word excerpt from a longer work.
            c. One chart, diagram, drawing, cartoon, or picture from a book or periodical.
        1.2.2   The copying is at the instance and inspiration of the moment, and the decision to use the work and the moment of its use for maximum effectiveness are so close in time that it would be unreasonable to expect a timely reply to request for permission.
        1.2.3   Cumulative effect
            a. The copied material is for use in only one course.

> b. Not more than one short work or two excerpts may be copied from the work of the same author, nor more than three excerpts from the same collective work or periodical volume during a school term.
>
> c. There shall not be more than nine instances of such multiple copying for one course during a school term.
>
> 1.2.4 A notice of copyright shall be included on each copy. (Note: Prohibitions in 1.2.3.b and 1.2.3.c above do not apply to current news periodicals or newspapers and current news sections of other periodicals.)

2. Those who wish to duplicate copyrighted works to a greater degree or quantity than allowed in the guidelines under section 1 must first obtain permission from the copyright owner. It is the responsibility of the individual to seek and obtain clearance from copyright owners prior to duplication. University staff will not make copies of copyrighted material outside the guidelines without knowledge that a clearance has been granted.

3. Notwithstanding the allowable copying noted in section 1 above, the following prohibitions must be observed:

    3.1. Copying shall not be used to create or to replace or substitute for anthologies, compilations, collective works or any non-print media.

    3.2. There shall be no copying of works intended to be consumable, such as workbooks, exercises, standardized tests and test booklets and answer sheets.

    3.3. Copying shall not substitute for the purchase of books, non-print media, publisher's reprints or periodicals; shall not be directed by higher authority, and shall not be repeated with respect to the same item by the same faculty member from term to term.

    3.4. Duplication of copyrighted motion picture films, slides, audio cassettes, phonograph records, or videotapes is prohibited except as allowed in the University Policy for Media Reproduction.

    3.5. No charge shall be made to the student beyond the actual cost of photocopying.

Distribution: Faculty & Staff

APPENDIX II

Humboldt State University Library
ONCORES
Online Course Reserve System

FOR STUDENTS	FOR FACULTY
SEARCH the ONCORES Online Course Reserve System (restricted to HSU students/faculty/staff) *Using ONCORES* A Student Guide to the Online Course Reserve System *Accessing ONCORES* A quick guide to accessing the system	*ABOUT* the ONCORES Online Course Reserve System *Introducing ONCORES* A Brief Slide Show Presentation About ONCORES *FAQ* about the ONCORES Online Course Reserve System *ONCORES Reserve Request Form* (HSU faculty use only)

Send comments and suggestions about this page to:
oncores@library.humboldt.edu

Last Updated: April 10, 2000

Links Checked: April 10, 2000

Humboldt State University I Library I Site Search I Catalyst I Subject Guides I Databases
The Library, Humboldt State University, Arcata, California 95521
Telephone: 707- 826-3441 Fax: 707- 826-3440

APPENDIX III

Humboldt State University Library
Searching the ONCORES
Online Course Reserve System

PLEASE NOTE: ARTICLES THAT WERE ONLINE FOR SPRING 2000 AND SUMMER 2000 HAVE BEEN ARCHIVED. ARTICLES FOR FALL 2000 are being processed, and we will begin posting them the week of August 21. If there are questions, send email to camozzij@laurel.humboldt.edu.

Departments using ONCORES:
Anthropology
Biology
English
Geography
History
Journalism & Mass Communications
Kinesiology
NRPI
Nursing
Political Science
Psychology
Secondary Education
Social Work
Wildlife

Send comments and suggestions about this page to:
oncores@library.humboldt.edu

Last Updated: August 26, 2000

Links Checked: August 29, 2000

Humboldt State University | Library | Site Search | Catalyst | Subject Guides | Databases
The Library, Humboldt State University, One Harpst St.,
Arcata, California 95521
Telephone: 707-826-3441   Fax: 707-826-3440

APPENDIX IV

Humboldt State University Library
Using ONCORES
A Student Guide to the Online Course Reserve System

Through ONCORES, an Online Course Reserve System, the Humboldt State University Library provides HSU students with round-the-clock access to reserve materials as requested by the faculty. Materials are accessible over the World Wide Web (Internet) from a networked personal computer in any location via the HSU Library homepage, preferably using a graphical web browser such as Netscape or Internet Explorer. ONCORES files may include journal articles, book chapters, course syllabi, reading lists, lecture notes, examinations, problem sets, or links to other copyright-free web resources. The Library has developed a brief handout, ACCESSING ONCORES, to instruct students in how to access the system.

Passwords and Copyright
In accordance with University policy and U.S. copyright law, ONCORES files are password-protected to help ensure that they are used primarily by students enrolled in a particular class. *The instructor is responsible for providing the students in that class with the user name and password required to access the system.* Students should not share the ONCORES password with anyone not enrolled in that class.

A copyright statement is included at the beginning of all copyright-protected materials in ONCORES. Students are advised to read that statement and use ONCORES materials accordingly. It is important to note that ONCORES files are intended for the personal academic use of the HSU community.

Technical Information
Most ONCORES documents are served in either HTML (hypertext markup language) or Adobe Acrobat PDF (portable document format), as specified by the instructor. Documents in HTML format are readily usable from a graphical web browser without need for additional software or "plug-ins." PDF documents, however, require the client browser to be configured to run Adobe Acrobat Reader software, which is available free of charge from the Adobe web site. The HSU Interdisciplinary Computing Facilities operated by Academic Computing offer computers which are pre-configured to run Acrobat Reader with either Netscape or Internet Explorer.

Additional Information
Further information can be found at the ONCORES homepage and the
ONCORES Frequently Asked Questions page. Other questions, suggestions,
and comments should be forwarded to the e-mail address indicated below, or
you can stop by and speak with staff in the Library Reserves Office in Library
110 (behind the Circulation Desk), or call them at 826-4401.

Send comments and suggestions about this page to:
oncores@library.humboldt.edu

Last Updated: August 17, 1999

Links Checked: August 17, 1999

Humboldt State University I Library I Site Search I Catalyst I Subject Guides I Databases
The Library, Humboldt State University, Arcata, California 95521
Telephone: 707- 826-3441   Fax: 707- 826-3440

APPENDIX V

Humboldt State University Library
Accessing ONCORES

To access ONCORES (the Humboldt State University Library Online Course Reserve System) using Netscape, Internet Explorer, Lynx, or another World Wide Web browser:

1. Open the location for the HSU Library homepage at http://library.humboldt.edu.

2. Once on the main Library homepage, select ONCORES from the Quick Links on the left side of the screen to go to the ONCORES main menu.

3. From the ONCORES main menu, select SEARCH the ONCORES Online Course Reserve System (restricted to HSU students/faculty/staff).

4. At the ONCORES user name/password prompt, enter:

   User Name: oncores

   Password: [consult instructor for password]

5. Once you have gained access to the ONCORES system, follow the links to the appropriate material, by selecting the Department, Course Name/Number, Professor, and the Name of Item to retrieve.

Note on Format: Most ONCORES documents are in HTML format, which are readable from any web browser without additional software. If the selected document is in Adobe Acrobat PDF format, however, your browser will need to be configured to run the Acrobat Reader helper application. Acrobat Reader is available in all campus Academic Computing Labs. Acrobat Reader software can also be downloaded free-of-charge from the Adobe web site (http://www.adobe.com/prodindex/acrobat/readstep.html); a link to the Adobe site is available from the ONCORES page under the heading ABOUT the ONCORES Course Reserve System.

Note on Copyright: All copyright-protected materials include a statement on copyright restrictions, followed by the text of the document.

Note on Print Quality: The quality of onscreen print is largely dependent upon the clarity of copy submitted to the Reserve Office and the configuration of the client computer. Some text and images may not appear sharp on the screen, but will generally produce readable copy when printed out.

Send comments and suggestions about this page to:
  oncores@library.humboldt.edu

Last Updated: August 18, 1999

Links Checked: August 18, 1999

Humboldt State University I Library I Site Search I Catalyst I Subject Guides I Databases
The Library, Humboldt State University, Arcata, California 95521
Telephone: 707- 826-3441   Fax: 707- 826-3440

APPENDIX VI

Humboldt State University Library
About ONCORES
Online Course Reserve System

The HSU Library provides a locally developed Online Course Reserves System (ONCORES) for use by the campus community. ONCORES, which was implemented beginning with the Fall 1997 semester, is the culmination of a pilot project which the Library initiated during the Spring 1996 semester, working with selected members of the teaching faculty. Through this service students in participating classes may have round-the-clock access via the *HSU Library homepage* to many of the materials which an instructor places on reserve for outside reading. Materials included in ONCORES are password-protected to help ensure that they are used by the target audience, i.e., students enrolled in a particular class, in compliance with established fair use doctrine as embodied in Section 107 of the United States Copyright Act.

ONCORES Goals and Guidelines
The basic purpose of ONCORES is to provide enrolled HSU students with on-line access to course reserve materials over the World Wide Web, as requested by HSU faculty. Materials served through ONCORES may include, but are not limited to, journal articles, book chapters, course syllabi, reading lists, lecture notes, examinations, problem sets, or links to other copyright-free web resources.

Some of the advantages of using ONCORES to serve reserve materials include:

- Providing access to course reserve materials 24 hours a day, seven days a week;

- Offering simultaneous access to the same item to any number of students;

- Facilitating web access to reserve materials from an appropriately configured personal computer in any location, on or off campus;

- Offering students a single point-of-entry interface for all online reserve materials;

- Providing the capability for pages to be either downloaded or printed for personal offline use;

- Ensuring that materials are being made available in compliance with established copyright policy.

ONCORES services are available to all HSU teaching faculty for use in support of regular classes.

Most materials served through ONCORES are either copyright-free or served in accordance with established HSU policies on fair use. Copyright-protected materials can only be served outside of HSU fair use policy if the faculty member either holds the copyright on the work or has obtained permission from the copyright holder to so use that material.

ONCORES Services Available from the Library

Library staff are available to provide the following services through ONCORES:

- Retrieving materials, as available, from the HSU Library collection;
- Scanning print source materials into OCR (optical character recognition) format;
- Converting scanned OCR materials into HTML (hypertext mark-up language);
- Scanning and converting print materials into PDF (portable document format);
- Creating the necessary directory structure for the course section and faculty member;
- Forging the links from the course directory to the online HTML or PDF documents;
- Providing the campus community with assistance and logistical support in the use of the ONCORES system.

Technical Information

The Library has two dedicated scanning stations which staff use to create ONCORES documents. These stations have been loaded with special software for use in the creation of HTML and PDF documents. The Library is currently using OmniPage Pro 8.0 for OCR/HTML conversion, and Adobe Acrobat 3.0 for creating PDF documents. HTML documents created with TextBridge can be viewed with any current generation web browser, but PDF documents require that a client computer be configured with special viewing software. This software, Adobe Acrobat Reader, is available free of charge from the Adobe web site.

Copyright and Fair Use

Materials included in ONCORES are made available in compliance with the *Humboldt State University Copying Policy,* and with established fair use provisions of the United States Copyright Act. In order to provide protections for copyright holders, while extending access to reserve materials in support of the academic mission of the University, all copyright-protected ONCORES materials feature:

A *Copyright Statement*—the following statement is included at the beginning of all copyright-protected materials served through ONCORES:

"WARNING CONCERNING COPYRIGHT RESTRICTIONS. The copyright law of the United States (Title 17, United States Code) governs the making of photocopies or other reproduction of copyrighted material. Under certain conditions specified in the law, libraries and archives are authorized to furnish a photocopy or other reproduction. One of the specified conditions is that the photocopy or reproduction is not to be used for any purpose other than private study, scholarship, or research. If electronic transmission of reserve material is used for purposes in excess of what constitutes 'fair use,' that user may be liable for copyright infringement."

Password Protection—all ONCORES materials are password-protected.

Access by Course/Instructor's Name—once access to ONCORES has been gained through use of the appropriate user name and password, specific reserve materials are organized by course number and instructor name.

Full Bibliographic Attribution—a complete bibliographic citation, including author, title, date, source, page numbers, etc., is included at the beginning of all copyright-protected materials.

ONCORES Request Form

Faculty may request online course reserve services by submitting an ONCORES Request Form to staff in the Library Reserve Office by e-mail, campus mail, or in-person.

Additional Information

Further information can be found at the ONCORES Frequently Asked Questions page. Forward other questions, suggestions, and comments to the e-mail address indicated below, or to the Library Reserve Office in Library 110 (behind the Circulation Desk).

Send comments and suggestions about this page to:
oncores@library.humboldt.edu

Last Updated: July 17, 2000

Links Checked: July 17, 2000

APPENDIX VII

Humboldt State University Library
ONCORES
Online Course Reserve System Frequently Asked Questions

Q: What is ONCORES?

A: Staff of the HSU Library developed ONCORES, or Online Course Reserve System, to provide HSU students with access to course reserve materials over the World Wide Web.

Q: What are the advantages of using ONCORES to serve reserve materials, as opposed to traditional print reserves?

A: ONCORES provides the following advantages over print reserves:

Accessibility—reserve materials are accessible over the Web 24 hours a day, seven days a week from any location;

Availability—reserve materials are always available, since they can never be checked out to another student or misplaced;

Increased readership—offering reserve materials through ONCORES may be expected to increase readership, since the materials are more readily available;

Convenient use—reserve materials may be printed out or downloaded for personal offline use.

Q: Why should a faculty member use ONCORES when the same material can be provided from their personal web page?

A: There are several distinct advantages to using ONCORES for both the faculty member and student:

Library staff do virtually all of the work once a reserve item has been identified. These services include retrieving a document (as available) from the Library collection, scanning and converting it to either HTML (hypertext mark-up language) or PDF (portable document format), creating the web directories, and forging the necessary links;

Library staff are available to provide logistical support, training, and consultation to both faculty and students, as needed to foster the effective use of the system;

ONCORES offers the student "one-stop shopping" for electronic reserve materials, regardless of course or instructor;

Library staff ensure that copyright-protected materials are afforded the safeguards provided for in the United States Copyright Act, and that those materials are served in accordance with applicable University policy.

Q: What sorts of materials may be placed on reserve through ONCORES?

A: Faculty may place both copyright-protected and non-copyrighted works on ONCORES. Access to copyright-protected works is provided in compliance with the same fair use guidelines which the Library applies to print reserve materials, unless the faculty member has specifically obtained clearance from the copyright holder to serve the work electronically. Non-copyrighted materials which can be offered through ONCORES without restriction include, but are not limited to, course syllabi, lecture notes, reading lists, solution sets, examinations, etc. Hyperlinks can also be forged from ONCORES to copyright-free Internet sites, such as, for example, a faculty member's web page.

Q: How can I access ONCORES?

A: ONCORES can be accessed by an appropriately configured personal computer via the *HSU Library homepage,* using the required user name and password provided to ONCORES participants. Virtually any current generation computer, configured to run a graphical web browser such as Netscape or Internet Explorer, should be able to access ONCORES files. Client computers will also need to have Adobe Acrobat Reader software (available free of charge from the *Adobe web site)* to view any documents in PDF format.

Q: Which electronic formats are supported by ONCORES?

A: Presently, most ONCORES documents are served in either HTML or PDF format. HTML is the recommended format for text documents with few graphics. PDF is recommended for works which contain graphical representations, such as charts, maps, tables, graphs, pictures, plates, etc., since it retains the actual image of the source document. It should be noted that PDF documents, which must be viewed using Acrobat Reader software, require a graphical user interface. Faculty interested in serving their materials in other formats should consult with ONCORES staff in the Library.

Q: What is the turnaround time for getting reserve materials into ONCORES?

A: Library staff make reserve materials available as quickly as possible, but turnaround will vary depending upon the time of year and the number of requests in the queue. As with all reserve materials, faculty are advised to submit their requests as early as they can. This is even more important with

ONCORES, since the scanning and conversion process can be quite labor-intensive and time-consuming. Faculty members can also help minimize turnaround time by providing the Library with the original source document, or a serviceable photocopy, at the time the reserve request is submitted.

Q: Why can't I access the articles in the ONCORES system by author or title?

A: Since most of the copyright-protected journal articles and book chapters in ONCORES are provided under fair use guidelines, the directory structure has been designed to limit the number of access points, while serving the class for which the readings are intended. As a result, direct author or title search keys are not provided. One timesaving tip for students using ONCORES from their own computer: bookmark the instructor's ONCORES page on your web browser, so that you can jump to that page the next time you need to access an online reserve document for that class.

Q: How do I submit reserve materials for ONCORES?

A: HSU faculty may submit items for ONCORES treatment by completing an *ONCORES Request Form* and forwarding it either electronically, by campus mail, or in-person to the Library Reserve Office located in Library 110 (behind the Circulation Desk). Faculty are strongly encouraged to provide the original source material (preferred), or a high-quality photocopy, to help ensure that the online version of the document will be satisfactory. At faculty request, Library staff can also retrieve available items from the Library collection for inclusion in ONCORES. Due to the additional work involved, however, such retrieval will add to the turnaround time for getting those materials online.

Q: Where can I find more information about ONCORES?

A: Further information can be found at the *ONCORES homepage,* or by contacting ONCORES staff in the Library Reserve Office in Library 110 (behind the Circulation Desk) by e-mail, in-person, or telephone at 826-4401.

Send comments and suggestions about this page to:
oncores@library.humboldt.edu

Last Updated: August 17, 1999

Links Checked: August 17, 1999

APPENDIX VIII

Humboldt State University Library
ONCORES
RESERVE REQUEST FORM

A faculty member must submit a reserve request form for each item they wish to have treated through *ONCORES*. Students should *SEARCH* ONCORES for access to materials already in the system. Refer to *ONCORES Frequently Asked Questions* for additional information about ONCORES services. Once completed, this form may be sent to the Library by e-mail, or printed out and forwarded to the Library Reserve Office, Library 110, via campus mail. (Do not use this form for print reserve requests).

Requestor Information
Instructor's Name:
Department/Course Number:
Telephone Number:
E-mail Address:
Date(s) Needed: through

Bibliographic Information (complete as applicable)
Author:
Title:
Publisher:
Publication Date:
Chapter/Page Nos.:
Journal Title:
Issue Information:
Format:
URL:
Call No.:

Notes on Completing Reserve Request Form
    Author: include the full name of the author of the book, journal article, etc., last name first.

Title: include the full title of the book, journal article, etc.

Publisher: if a book, include the name of the publisher.

Publication Date: if a book, indicate date of publication.

Chapter/Page Nos.: if a book, indicate the chapter heading and/or inclusive page numbers of citation.

Journal Title: if a journal, indicate the complete journal title.

Issue Information: if a journal, indicate the issue numeration, date, and page numbers of article.

Format: specify the electronic format to be used for the document, i.e., HTML (hypertext mark-up language) or PDF (portable document format).

URL: if a hyperlink to another web resource is being requested, provide the complete URL (uniform resource locator) for the resource.

Call No.: specify the call number only if the item is held by the Library and the faculty member is requesting that Library staff retrieve the item from the collection for ONCORES treatment.

Note: If the material being cited is in the Library collection and available at the time the request is received, Library staff will use the call number supplied on this form to retrieve and copy that item for conversion to ONCORES. If the item is either not in the collection, or unavailable at the time the request is received, the faculty member should make provisions to provide a copy from another source. Library staff will make every effort to get materials into ONCORES quickly. To help keep turnaround time to a minimum, faculty are strongly encouraged to provide the source material whenever possible, but especially when the online reserve material is needed on short notice.

Send comments and suggestions about this page to:
oncores@library.humboldt.edu.

Links Checked: August 26, 1999

6

OSCR: Open Source Software and Electronic Reserves

W. GROTOPHORST and J. FRUMKIN

WHAT IS OPEN SOURCE SOFTWARE?

Open source software (OSS) is not only a type of software, but a type of software created using a particular philosophy. Sometimes known as free software (free as in Freedom of Information Act, as opposed to free as in free beer), OSS promotes the ability to read, understand, modify, and enhance the source code of the software, in addition to allowing for the open and free use of software. This provides the ability to produce software in a way that better meets the needs of the end user and allows the end user a level of self-support that isn't available through commercial products.

OSS is defined as a tool and a philosophy that "promotes software reliability and quality by supporting independent peer review and rapid evolution of source code. To be certified as open source, the license of a program must guarantee the right to read, redistribute, modify, and use it freely."[1] By guaranteeing access to the source code of a program and the freedom to modify that code, OSS software can be customized, evolved, and improved to meet the specialized needs of users. Basically, OSS is software that continuously goes through the peer-review process.

This works very effectively. Some examples of open source software are Linux (a popular operating system), Apache (the most popular web server in use today), Perl (the most widely used programming/scripting language for the Web), and BIND (the Internet tool that ties together domain names and IP addresses). Without OSS, the Internet would not exist as it does today. OSS allows anyone to learn about the workings of the software itself. How important is this? Well, if you had to learn to produce an HTML page for the first time, how might you go about doing so? Perhaps you would look at someone else's web page and then click "show source" on your browser. One reason the World Wide Web has grown so quickly is that web pages are virtually open source pieces of code themselves (true, there is no inherent license that goes along with an HTML page, but for every page that is viewable by a browser, the source code is also available for viewing). The ability to learn from the source code and then build upon that code makes OSS not only a peer-review process, but a peer-contributing process as well.

OPEN SOURCE AND LIBRARIES

How does OSS relate to libraries? Currently, there are some forty-two distinct projects addressing such items as Z39.50 clients and servers, integrated library systems, MARC utilities, customizable user interfaces for online public access catalogs (OPACs), etc. (A list of most of these projects can be found at www.oss4lib.org/projects.) Libraries have vast needs in the new information world; many of our traditional services are moving into the digital realm, but, unfortunately, our tools aren't always keeping up with our needs. Part of this is due to the rapid change of the information landscape; much of it is due to the more recent reliance of libraries on outside vendors to take the lead on innovation when it comes to information organization and access technology.

Traditionally, libraries have been leaders and innovators when it comes to providing access to information; however, in the last twenty years, we have given up much of that role to library-related vendors and companies, which in some cases is effective, but in many cases is not. Occasionally, libraries will build homegrown tools and systems, but this option is often prohibitive because of the high cost of not only creating the actual software, but also maintaining it. However, by combining resources and using the strong community that libraries have already built, we can use open source methods and tools to pool our development and support resources so that libraries can once again be the creators and innovators of the tools we use. OSCR, developed initially at

George Mason University and released as open source software, is allowing many institutions to collaborate and contribute to the development of an advanced, customizable electronic reserve system.

OSCR:
OPEN SOURCE COURSE RESERVES

Applying technology to the task of managing a course reserve service is not quite as new as the current interest in e-reserves might suggest. Since at least the early eighties, there have been course reserve modules in library management systems, and their capabilities have evolved and improved over time. Today, while quite good at tracking reserve materials, few of these vendor-supplied solutions actually provide for the delivery of digital content. Most vendors consider this delivery function an add-on and market the expanded capability as a "digital archive system" or some other similarly positioned product.

As might be expected, this gap between what vendors offer in their base package and what libraries feel they need is being bridged in many libraries by in-house developers. In a recent survey by the Association of Research Libraries (ARL) over half of the respondents providing electronic reserves were doing so via a homegrown, web-based product.[2] While many of these locally developed systems are so tightly focused on meeting a local need that they are not readily transferable, we are beginning to see systems that have a more extensible design.

Open Source Course Reserve is one such homegrown package, developed from the ground up to provide a scalable, easily managed, electronic reserve system. Distributed as open source (timesync.gmu. edu/OSCR), the OSCR system is constructed with freely available software tools and provides an inexpensive but nevertheless robust option for those sites with development talent available in-house. With source code provided, OSCR can also be used as a departure point for those institutions interested in developing a system of their own.

System Features

We began work on OSCR with a relatively small list of must-have design goals, the majority of which were driven by our experience developing other small library-related systems:

- web based (to eliminate client software issues)
- scalable (successful projects always seem to grow)
- fast (we cannot always throw more hardware at it)
- low maintenance (we are often understaffed)
- support delivery of PDF files (pure image files are too large and OCR/text is not a viable alternative)

As we discussed implementation, it was suggested that we could meet our initial needs with a series of static web pages—one per professor's course. Admittedly, this would enable us to fast-track the project, but the downstream costs would be enormous (we would dread seeing the next semester roll around with hundreds of web pages needing updates). Still looking for ways to jump-start the process, we next considered using a formatted flat file and a CGI process—a file listing the articles for each course and a CGI process that searched it in real time and formatted the results as an HTML page. This would have eliminated the drudgery of HTML coding that our first approach promised, but it would not have scaled well and there would have been quite a bit of redundant data entry (as more than one course might use a particular reading). Paradoxically, we finally realized that moving to a more complicated system architecture would actually help us simplify the product.

Already familiar with MySQL (having used it to produce a database of databases for our library web site), we began to design a system built on an SQL database. This increased the difficulty of our initial implementation, but we expected to be rewarded with increased scalability, better accuracy in our data, higher performance, data reusability, and enhanced reliability of the system. Our first task was deciding on a structure for our database.

Database Architecture

It is worth taking a few moments to consider OSCR's internal structure, not only to understand how OSCR works, but also to see how one models a real-world activity like e-reserves in a relational database.

A brief aside on terminology for those new to databases: A database is made up of one or more tables. Each table has a name and consists of columns (fields) and rows (records)—think of a spreadsheet.

All the information in the database is stored in these tables. Ideally, the same piece of information never appears in more than one table (except where it must for table-linking purposes).

Read more than a few paragraphs on relational database theory and you will encounter the principle that tables are supposed to represent things in the real world, and that each table should represent just one thing. E-reserves, it seems, is really concerned with just two things—articles (readings, web links, etc.) and courses. Accordingly, we should be able to adequately model it with a database containing two tables—one for the courses and one for the readings. Of course, a database is more than just a description of the tables it contains—the relationships between the tables are also important.

There are three types of relationships between any two tables: one-to-one, one-to-many, and many-to-many. Consider a two-table database. In a one-to-one relationship, for every row in the first table, there is at most one row in the second table (this is relatively rare). Much more common is the one-to-many relationship, where for each row in the first table there are zero, one, or many rows in the second table. It might seem that our OSCR system would show such a relationship between the course and article tables (one course could have zero, one, or many corresponding entries in the article table), but it is a bit more complicated (see fig. 1). Yes, there will be multiple article records that relate to a particular course record, but one might also expect to find multiple course records using the same record in the article table. Thus, the course and article tables in the OSCR system have a many-to-many

FIGURE 1   OSCR is built on three tables

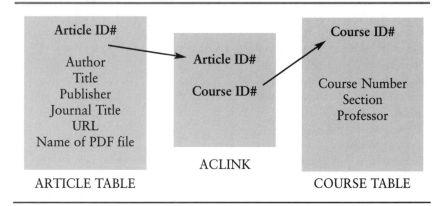

relationship. Database theory says such a relationship between two tables requires a third linking table. For OSCR, we call it the ACLINK (for article/course link) table.

This structure offers several immediate benefits. First, it is simple and speeds up our search function because the CGI process need only search the ACLINK table looking for the course we need; searches on smaller tables are faster (see fig. 2). Second, since our article table is now independent of any particular course, we need to enter information about an article only once. If a second course (or the same course next semester) needs the same article, we simply create a new record in

FIGURE 2   The OSCR tables described

Article

Field	Type	Null	Key	Default	Extra
articleID	int(1) unsigned zerofill		PRI	0	
title	char(150)		MUL		
authorFirstName	char(35)		PRI		
authorLastName	char(40)		PRI		
authorMiddleInitial	char(25)		PRI		
location	char(40)		MUL		
articleURL	char(200)	YES		NULL	
size	int(1) unsigned	YES		NULL	
journalName	char(100)				
journalVolume	int(1) unsigned zerofill	YES		NULL	
journalNumber	int(1) unsigned zerofill	YES		NULL	
journalMonth	char(12)	YES		NULL	
journalYear	char(9)	YES		NULL	
ownedByTheLibrary	tinyint(1) unsigned zerofill	YES		NULL	
MultipleAuthors	char(128)	YES		NULL	
journalPages	char(20)	YES		NULL	
flag1	char(2)	YES		NULL	
isbook	char(1)	YES		NULL	
bookeditionnote	char(25)	YES		NULL	
bookpublisherstring	char(100)	YES		NULL	
displaynote	char(160)	YES		NULL	
dataentrynote	char(80)	YES		NULL	

ACLINK—linking the course with the article information we already have in our article table. Finally, when a term ends, we simply break the links in the ACLINK table and start linking anew. Over time, the amount of work decreases as we begin to leverage the data entry done for articles that reappear from semester to semester. We use a flag in the ACLINK table to show whether a link is active (current) and in this way preserve historic information when the link is broken (set inactive).

Course

Field	Type	Null	Key	Default	Extra
semesterID	char(6)		PRI		
coursePrefix	char(10)		PRI		
courseNumber	char(6)		PRI		
courseName	char(80)				
sectionNumber	char(5)		PRI		
instructorLastName	char(40)				
instructorFirstName	char(40)				
instructorMiddleInitial	char(25)				
password	char(12)	YES		NULL	
opacLinkURL	char(200)	YES		NULL	
opacLinkOn	char(1)	YES		NULL	

ACLINK

Field	Type	Null	Key	Default	Extra
articleID	int(1) unsigned zerofill		PRI	0	
authorFirstName	char(35)		PRI		
authorLastName	char(35)		PRI		
authorMiddleInitial	char(25)		PRI		
semesterID	char(6)		PRI		
coursePrefix	char(10)		PRI		
courseNumber	char(6)		PRI		
sectionNumber	char(5)		PRI		
active	char(1)			Y	

System Architecture

OSCR is perhaps best viewed as a systems integration project, the internal cohesion supplied by a bit of Perl coding. With the exception of the CGI scripts, the system is really nothing more than the combination of several open source components. We use the freely available Apache web server (www.apache.org), Perl (www.cpan.org), MySQL (www.mysql.com), and the Perl DBI (database interface) module (www.cpan.org). For Linux developers, AbriaSoft has just released a CD-ROM that includes these four components (as well as PHP) in a single, easy-to-install RPM package (www.abriasoft.com).

We have not attempted a Windows NT/2000 version of OSCR, but each of these packages is available on that platform as well. Pascal V. Calarco at Virginia Commonwealth University has ported (and no doubt improved upon) OSCR to ColdFusion and the Windows NT/2000 platform (see his discussion in chapter 8).

How It Works

From the beginning we decided to build a system that could scale far beyond any demand we anticipated and one that could support intense, sustained activity. Accordingly, we designed an architecture that could be split among several servers. In our original implementation, we put a web server, Perl, and the MySQL database on one UNIX machine and a web server and our PDF files on another. In this way, we split the load: one server queried the database and built web pages of links for users while the other delivered the PDF files once the user clicked on his choice. After one semester we realized this was not necessary and combined all components on a single machine.

Figure 3 shows a typical interaction from the user's point of view.

1. When a user clicks on the "Search E-reserves Link," a CGI process scans the database in real time and builds an HTML menu page listing all courses and all professors. The user selects professor, course, or both from the drop-down boxes and hits submit. Using a CGI process to build the search screen in real time means that as soon as an article or course is entered into the system it is available to end users.
2. The web server runs a CGI process (OSCRsearch.cgi) that queries the MySQL server, asking for matching information.

FIGURE 3   The OSCR system

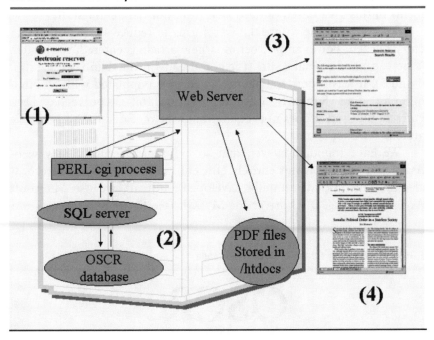

The CGI process then builds a web page of results and sends it back to the user.

3. To retrieve the actual article, the user clicks on the small icon that accompanies each entry in the list. If the article is a PDF file, the icon is a small Acrobat logo; web links offer a small WWW icon.

4. The web server retrieves the PDF file from its document root and sends it along to the user.

Data Entry

The OSCR system requires a fair amount of data entry—particularly at the start of an e-reserve service. We use web-based forms for data entry and thus are able to enforce certain normalization rules (e.g., capitalization rules, checking validity of selected data elements, etc.) before a record enters the database. We are continuously looking for ways to streamline the data entry process and recently made many improvements in this area based on feedback from our data entry staff.

We are also able to use the web forms to reduce some of the data entry burden. For example, before a new article is entered, the system is first scanned to make sure it is not already in the database (see figs. 4 and 5). If it is found, the data entry form is populated with all bibliographic data. Similarly, once information for a course has been entered, the system does not require that it be repeated for every article attached to that course.

We have found, however, that so far implementing a fully web-based edit module is not entirely efficient (at least not the one-record-at-a-time method we initially developed). Instead, we use Microsoft Access with an ODBC driver for MySQL (see fig. 6). This allows our

FIGURE 4   Opening screen of OSCR staff mode

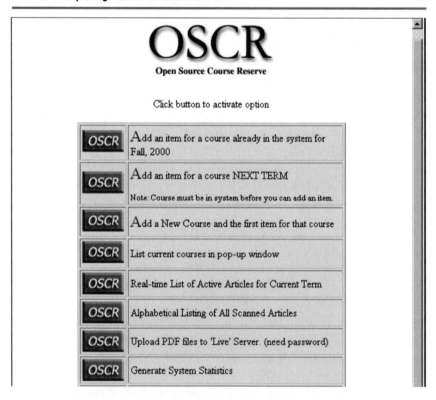

FIGURE 5 Step one in adding an article is clicking on the course

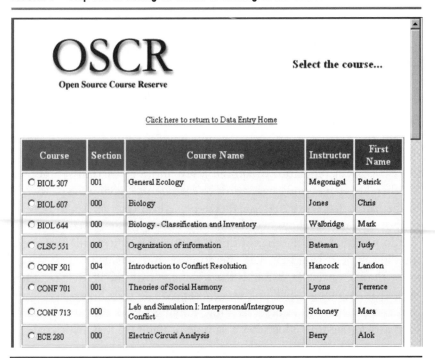

FIGURE 6 The OSCR database under Microsoft Access (using MySQL ODBC driver)

articleID	title	authorFirstNam	authorLastNam
34	Rules, Discretion and Reputation In a Model	Robert	Barro
35	Volatility tests and efficient markets	John	Cochrane
36	Do Long-Term Interest Rates Overreact to Sh	N	Mankiw
37	Why Do Banks Need a Central Bank?	C	Goodhart
0	Cooperation, Harassment, and Involuntary Ur	Assar	Lindbeck
39	New Classical Macroeconomics: A Sympath	Bennett	McCallum
40	Real Business Cycles	John	Long Jr.
41	Time to Build and Aggregate Fluctuations	Finn	Kydland
42	Market Structure and Macroeconomic Fluctu	Robert	Hall
69	Cold Facts About the "Hot hand" in Basketba	Thomas	Gilovich
68	Asset Bubbles and Overlapping Generations	Jean	Tirole
67	Credit Rationing in Markets with Imperfect Inf	Andrew	Weiss
46	Implementation Cycles	Andrei	Shleifer
47	Mutual Banks and Stock Banks	Eric	Rasmusen
48	Industrialization and the Big Push	Robert	Vishny
49	Dividend Variability and Variance Bounds Tes	Terry	Marsh
50	Rules Rather Than Discretion: The Inconsiste	Edward	Prescott

data entry staff to use the web forms for initial entry of data but view the entire database under Access when making corrections or modifications. Work is under way to improve web-based editing, and that capability should be better supported in a future release.

Security/Copyright Compliance

In the first year of operation (1997), we restricted access to our OSCR system to those physically on the university's network (or coming in through a validated proxy server). Over time, we began to feel that perhaps copyright regulations required a few more restrictions on access. We then began assigning passwords to each course, giving the password to the instructor when materials were placed on reserve. Today, OSCR supports course-level passwords that are stored within the course table. We do not track the number of times an article is downloaded (viewed) for the simple reason that that operation occurs outside the OSCR system—that is, once OSCR builds the web page with the PDF links, it has no way of knowing which link was chosen. We do distribute a Perl script that can process the web server's log, tallying successful downloads of each article. Figure 7 illustrates a sample of one OSCR statistics page.

OSCR IN COLLABORATION:
THE UNIVERSITY OF ARIZONA LIBRARY

The University of Arizona (UA) Library's electronic reserve service began in 1998. Initially, the UA Library did not use any specific system for implementing electronic reserves; articles were scanned and then placed on a server in a directory that related to the instructor's name and the course title. While this approach proved the easiest to implement, it had a number of drawbacks, including a high level of upkeep and maintenance. These problems only increased as the amount of reserve materials and the number of classes using electronic reserves increased; i.e., the bare-bones approach did not scale well.

The UA Library decided to look for and implement an electronic reserves system. Much like George Mason University, we had several requirements and issues with which to deal. And, like George Mason, we found that current commercial products could not meet our needs sufficiently. However, instead of starting from scratch to build our own

FIGURE 7   Excerpt of system statistics OSCR produces on the fly

OSCR

Open Source Course Reserve

Number of Articles stored on the system: 2735

Number of active articles in system for Fall, 2000 session: 0

Number of URL links in system: 82

Articles by Course / 2000F

Course	# articles
ANTH 399 Section 000	8
ARIN 307 Section 001	7
ARTH 101 Section 000	3
ARTH 371 Section 001	1
ARTS 307 Section 001	2
BIOL 307 Section 000	10
BIOL 377 Section 001	27
BIOL 550 Section 000	3
BIOL 568 Section 001	14

system, we were able to implement the OSCR code. Not only did this allow us to implement a user-oriented, customizable system, but it also allowed us to use our resources to further the development of OSCR and to spend time on higher-level features that might not have been possible had we chosen to collaborate via the open source model.

Our implementation of OSCR is very similar to the original at George Mason. The core infrastructure, such as the database tables and code design, is the same. We updated some of the code and added features, some that were to meet specific UA Library needs, and some that might be useful to other institutions implementing OSCR. One of the UA Library's unique requirements was that our electronic reserve system needed to work seamlessly with POLIS, a campus instructional tool that gives instructors an easy way to create a course web site. One of POLIS's features is its ability to display a course's electronic reserve content (see fig. 8). We were able to add the ability for instructors, through POLIS, to not only have their students retrieve course reserve materials, but also to submit their citation information directly into the database via POLIS. Having instructors directly enter citation information reduced the staff workload tremendously.

FIGURE 8   POLIS

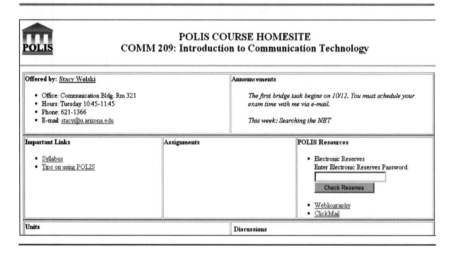

Another feature of POLIS that we worked on adding was web-based editing of both course and article information. Although instructors could enter the citations for their courses directly, we still needed an easy mechanism to then add the proper PDF link or URL once the production staff processed the material for the course. We also needed the ability to edit course and article information without having to access the database directly. So we added forms for staff to be able to edit article and course information (see fig. 9). Having the staff go through web forms to edit information protects the database's overall integrity; staff cannot accidentally delete large portions of the data, and when an article is updated or deleted, data are changed in all appropriate tables, as needed.

All of the coding done at the UA Library has been sent back to George Mason University for checking and deciding which pieces might be useful to include in future releases of OSCR.

FIGURE 9   Web-based editing form

Title	Author Middle Name	Author First Name	Author Last Name	Article Link	PDF File Name	Citation
○ Asking Questions About Communication (pp.27-37)	-	L.	Frey	-	wolski/comm280/f01aski.pdf	Frey, L., Botan, C., & Kreps, G. (2000). Asking Questions About Communication. In Investigating Communication: An Introduction To Research Methods, 2nd. Ed.
○ Asking Questions About Communication (pp.38-47)	-	L.	Frey	-	wolski/comm280/f01aski2.pdf	Frey, L., Botan, C., & Kreps, G. (2000). Asking Questions About Communication. I
○ Computers And Privacy	-	-	Johnson	-	wolski/comm209/f02comp.pdf	-
○ On The Study Of Technology And Task: A Variable-based Approach	-	-	Nass	-	wolski/comm209/f17vari.pdf	-
○ Telltales And Overhearers	-	-	Pemberton	-	wolski/comm209/f01tell.pdf	-
○ The Beginning Of The Information Age	-	B.	Oates	-	wolski/comm209/f03begi.pdf	Chapter 2
○ The Role Of The Change Agent And The Consequences Of Innovation, Pages 254-265	-	-	Rogers	-	wolski/comm209/f01role.pdf	-
○ The Role Of The Change Agent And The Consequences Of Innovation, pages 266-283	-	-	Rogers	-	wolski/comm209/f01role2.pdf	-
○ Truthtelling-a Case Study Of Electronically Altered Photographs	G.	C.	Christians	-	wolski/comm209/f12trut.pdf	-

In this way, we hope that our work on OSCR here helps in the development of OSCR as a whole, and we look forward to seeing and implementing what others contribute to the system.

FUTURE DIRECTIONS

We have several goals for OSCR development, not the least of which is to increase the number of sites employing the software. Many of the system's best features have resulted from suggestions or contributions from other users. As other sites extend the program, current and future users can benefit from their modifications. Some possible future developments may be an extension or redesign of the underlying data model so that XML import/export features can be implemented. Another evolution of OSCR may include the development of an API so that the OSCR system can be easily integrated with our campus systems, such as an institution's ILS. Other developments will take place with OSCR—many of which we cannot even foresee today. Because OSCR is open source, many of the future developments will happen at institutions implementing the software. The open source philosophy—the philosophy of technological advancement through sharing, peer perusal, and modification of source code—is increasingly popular, and OSCR seems to fit squarely within that tradition.

NOTES

1. Daniel Chudnov, Open Source Systems for Libraries: Getting Started (www.oss4lib.org/readings/oss4lib-getting-started.php), 1999.
2. Cindy Kristof, "Electronic Reserves Operations in ARL Libraries," SPEC Kit 245 (Washington, D.C.: Association of Research Libraries, 1999).

7

Copyright Considerations for Electronic Reserves

LAURA N. GASAWAY

L ibrarians have long been aware that reserve collections raise important copyright concerns. Whether the library paid much attention to these concerns was often balanced against the need to maintain reserve collections for its users in order to provide quality services and ensure the availability of course materials. The copyright issues were simpler when reserve collections consisted of original volumes, videotapes, etc. Incorporation of photocopies of articles and book chapters, reproduced audio and videotapes, and duplicated computer software set the stage for complicated copyright issues and disputes between librarians and publishers. Still, some libraries paid little attention to copyright although others followed the American Library Association's Model Policy closely.[1]

The advent of electronic reserves has again focused attention on copyright issues as one of the important elements that must be taken into account when planning, establishing, and maintaining electronic reserves. Moreover, many libraries find themselves having to explain copyright to faculty and members and often advocating for copyright holders and defending the library's attempt to comply with the law.

An earlier version of this article appeared as "Library Reserve Collections: From Paper to Electronic Collections," in *Growing Pains: Adapting Copyright for Libraries, Education, and Society,* ed. Laura Gasaway (Littleton, Colo.: Fred Rothman, 1997), 125.

COPYRIGHT AND TRADITIONAL RESERVE COLLECTIONS

Placing Original Volumes on Reserve

Before libraries had lending collections, the entire library, in effect, was a reserve collection. Since nothing left the library—all materials were used on site—there was no reason to create separate reserve collections during this era.

It is unclear when the first true reserve collections were created, but as libraries began to establish lending collections, the need to remove heavily used items from general circulation arose. When only a few novels and other types of general reading materials circulated, the need still was not great. But as nonfiction works began to circulate and demands on collections increased, libraries had to find ways to extend the use of a small number of copies of important works. Library funding has never been sufficient to permit the purchase of duplicate materials in unlimited copies, regardless of demand. At some point, libraries responded to this demand by removing works from the general circulating collection and placing them in a separate noncirculating collection or in one with a short circulation period. Initially, the books and materials placed on reserve were those the library identified as heavily used. Two purposes were served by creating a separate reserve collection: more users could have access to the work if the circulation period was made very short, and the materials themselves were protected. These collections were often referred to as "permanent reserves," indicating that the library had selected the materials to be placed on reserve and that it intended for the works to remain in the protected collection indefinitely.

In many academic institutions, one copy of each assigned textbook is placed on reserve in the library to assist students who forget their book on a particular day or who cannot afford to purchase the assigned text. Although textbooks were not necessarily part of the permanent reserve collection, they also were original works that were placed on reserve. To supplement textbooks assigned for specific courses, faculty members have long assigned additional readings. Sometimes these readings were required, and sometimes they could be reviewed for extra credit in the course. The faculty member provided a bibliography of these readings either separately or as a part of the course syllabus. In order to ensure the availability of these materials, they were placed in a reserve room or collection. These materials were usually called "temporary" or "course reserves."

Librarians often responded to temporary course demands by placing original volumes on reserve for the class term. For example, when a faculty member assigned a chapter of a book and the library determined that there was demand for the work, the volume was placed on reserve. This often included bound volumes of journals or a single volume from a set or from a multivolume treatise.

The first mention of a reserve room in library literature was in 1878, when Harvard College reported that professors commonly gave the library a list of books to which they intended to refer their students during the class term. The library would then remove these books from the circulating collection to preserve their use for the class.[2] A decade later, Melvil Dewey stated that many books were placed "behind the circulation desk in closed shelves" in some academic libraries. The reason for such restricted access was that students took the books and thereby denied access to others.[3] Writing in the 1930s, Charles Harvey Brown stated that reserve rooms are mainly a creation of the twentieth century. Interestingly, he also said there was some indication that the use of "defined reading" was decreasing and was being replaced by assignment of topics for investigation.[4] He described the gradual movement from closed to open shelves for reading rooms and cited Columbia University and Vassar as institutions that maintained open shelves in their reserve rooms. The University of Nebraska went from closed to open reserve shelves between 1902 and 1910.[5] Other libraries reported a combination of open and closed shelves for their reserves, and the University of Chicago even established a rental collection for reserve materials. For a "moderate fee" students could check out reserve materials and take them home. This system did not replace the reserve room but apparently did reduce the number of duplicate copies the library purchased.[6]

Photocopies on Reserve

Often a library had difficulty meeting the need for course reserves because it did not have enough copies of a work to satisfy the demand. Primarily for course reserves, libraries began to take advantage of reprography to make multiple copies of book chapters and articles that faculty members assigned to their students. These collections consisted of photocopies of articles and chapters placed on reserve at the request of an individual faculty member. The materials were almost always made available under the name of the course or the faculty member's name.

It is easy to think that reprography began in the early 1960s, when photocopiers began to appear in libraries. In discussing the fact that many academic libraries would not place periodical volumes on reserve unless duplicates were available, in 1933 the following statement appeared: "[I]f numbers are in print, additional copies are purchased. If the numbers are out of print, typed or photostatic copies of articles are made."[7] Also, if the material was rare or scarce, "sometimes certain sections of a rare book are photostated or mimeographed and duplicate pages are thus made available."[8] No mention was made of copyright. Reproducing articles and other works for reserve collection is not a new phenomenon, however.

A student who requests an item at the reserve desk has two options: either read the photocopy checked out at the reserve desk or make an additional copy of the photocopy to read later. Exactly what percentage of students make copies of the photocopied item is unknown, but practicing librarians believe it is high. Making a copy of a reserve item does not necessarily mean that the student reads the material. In fact, one recent study of reserve collections found that only 40 percent of the students in a class even retrieved items placed on reserve.[9] There was no indication of how many of the 40 percent *read* the item! Whether a student who makes a photocopy of a reserve item infringes copyright has long been debated, but most copyright experts believe that when a student photocopies an item for nonprofit educational use, it is either a fair use or a personal use that is permitted under copyright. Most agree that fair use applies as discussed below, but others believe that fair use does not even have to be applied because the use is a personal one.[10]

In recent years, there have been some reports of abuses of traditional photocopy reserve collections. For example, some faculty members began to put photocopies of all of the readings for a course on reserve and did not require students to purchase a textbook or other materials. Thus, reserve collections grew tremendously, and the original purpose of such collections was altered. Actually, complaints about abuse of reserve collections are not new. The following complaint was published in 1938:

In my humble judgment, some professors have simply lost their sense of proportion. They have become so enamored of the reserved book system that they feel they could not give their favorite course unless there were from 500–1,000 books on reserve, specifically ticketed with the name and number of their course.[11]

While this comment dealt with placing originals on reserve, librarians often made the same complaint about photocopied materials.

COPYRIGHT BASICS AND THE ALA MODEL POLICY

Traditional reserve collections in which only original volumes are placed into a special collection raise no copyright concerns for the library. In the United States, there is no restriction on the right to read, and copyright holders are not entitled to any royalties when books are loaned by libraries.[12] Under section 109(a) of the Copyright Act, anyone who possesses a copy of a work may dispose of that copy without any further royalties to the copyright holder. Called the first sale doctrine, this section of the statute permits libraries to loan works to users or even to rent them to library patrons. Thus, placing original works on reserve and loaning them to users is permitted under the first sale doctrine. Copyright concerns arise only when materials are *reproduced* for library reserve collections.

Copyright Basics

Under the Copyright Act of 1976, original works of authorship that are fixed in tangible media of expression are entitled to copyright protection.[13] Copyright holders get a bundle of rights: reproduction, distribution, adaptation, performance, display, and, for sound recordings, the right of digital transmission.[14] In reserve collections consisting wholly or in part of photocopied or digitized materials, it is the reproduction and distribution rights that are involved. When a library photocopies or scans articles and book chapters and places them on reserve, it has engaged in reproduction. In making the copies available to students who then check out the reproduced copies from the reserve collection, the library is not necessarily distributing that copy, however.

Distribution typically envisions a change in possession of the copy, but in the reserve collection situation, a student simply borrows the copy. That user may make a further photocopy, but the library's photocopy is returned to the library. Even if the distribution right is implicated along with the reproduction right, the library has not necessarily infringed the copyright.

The exclusive rights of the copyright holder are tempered by a number of limitations or exceptions found in the statute, the most important of which is fair use.[15] Often called the "safety valve" of copyright, fair use excuses activity that normally would be infringement. When a use is a fair use, the user does not have to seek permission from the copyright holder or pay royalties. The law simply recognizes that some uses of copyrighted works have social value and are excused. Section 107 of the Copyright Act provides that:

> [T]he fair use of a copyrighted work, including such use by reproduction in copies . . . for purposes such as criticism, comment, news reporting, teaching (including multiple copies for classroom use), scholarship, or research, is not an infringement of copyright . . .[16]

In order to determine whether a use is fair, the statute directs that the following factors be considered: (1) purpose and character of the use, (2) nature of the copyrighted work, (3) amount and substantiality used, and (4) effect on the potential market for or value of the work. One of the difficulties with fair use is that only a court can determine authoritatively whether a particular use is fair. Thus, it is not only a limitation on the exclusive rights of the copyright holder, but it is also a defense to copyright infringement.[17] There are no "bright line" rules for judging fair use, but there are some principles that can be used to help evaluate a particular use and whether it qualifies as a fair use. Courts balance these four factors in making a fair-use determination.

The first factor, *purpose and character of the use*, focuses on whether the use is for scholarship or commercial gain. Nonprofit educational uses generally are more likely to be a fair use than are commercial ones.[18] Courts also favor so-called productive or transformative uses over simple reproductions. A transformative use makes some contribution of new intellectual value, such as when a critic quotes extensively from a book in a literary criticism of the book.[19] Clearly, photocopying materials for reserve collections involves no such transformative use. The use, however, is for nonprofit educational purposes, so the use for reserve collections satisfies one prong of the first factor but not the other. This may be enough.

Nature of the copyrighted work, the second fair use factor, requires an examination of the copyrighted work itself. Thus, each work must be judged separately on this factor. The legislative history states that there is a definite difference between making a copy of a short news note and reproducing an entire musical score. Further, by their nature some works have no fair-use right; this includes standardized tests and work booklets, works that are meant to be consumed.[20] As a general rule, uses of factual works are more likely to be a fair use than are uses of creative works.[21] Other considerations for this factor include whether the work is unpublished or is out of print.[22] To rely on this factor in a fair-use determination for materials placed on reserve thus requires looking at each item individually.

The third factor, *amount and substantiality used,* focuses on how much of the copyrighted work is reproduced. Generally, the smaller the amount used, the more likely the use will be found to be fair. This quantitative determination is very dependent on how "the work" is defined. For example, section 108(d) states that libraries may reproduce a single copy of an article from a periodical issue or other contribution from a collective work for a user. This indicates that the copyrighted work is the journal issue, and certainly librarians had never considered otherwise until the *Texaco* decision held that the individual article was the copyrighted work.[23] Thus, outside of section 108, reproduction of an article may constitute copying 100 percent of a copyrighted work. Although short portions of a book might be used, it is unlikely that portions of articles would be placed on reserve; the entire article is generally duplicated and the reproduction is placed on reserve. The entire work is usually copied if the work is defined as an article or a separately authored chapter of a book.

Amount and substantiality is a qualitative test as well. If the alleged infringer takes the heart of the work, regardless of the amount used quantitatively, the use will not be a fair one. Determining the heart of a work is not difficult with some works, but it is very difficult with others. The classic example is a thirty-minute videotape of the eruption of a volcano, only one minute of which depicts the actual eruption. The remainder of the tape records events leading up to the eruption and then the aftermath. If the alleged infringer has reproduced the one-minute segment containing the actual eruption, he has copied only one-thirtieth of the tape, but that is the heart of the work and thus would not be a fair use.[24]

The final fair use factor, *market effect*, focuses on the effect of the use on the potential market for or value of the use. This is the economic test for the copyright holder. In *Harper & Row*, the Supreme Court indicated that the fourth factor was the most important one,[25] but it retracted from this position in *Acuff-Rose v. Campbell* when it held that no one factor was more important than another.[26]

Nonetheless, a series of cases indicates that publishers have an economic interest in the right to license to photocopy and that avoiding paying those royalties even for research and educational uses may not be a fair use. In *Texaco*, the Second Circuit Court of Appeals held that making single photocopies of articles from journals to which the library subscribed, at that Texaco facility by a scientist who archived the copies for later use, was not a fair use.[27] The archiving, the fact that the publishers had provided a mechanism for licensing through the Copyright Clearance Center, and the court's holding that the publishers had lost the right to license to photocopy because Texaco had opted not to pay royalties for these copies, meant that the use was not a fair one.[28] Two cases dealing with the reproduction of coursepacks for college courses by commercial photocopy services but at the request of a faculty member are *Basic Books, Inc. v. Kinko's Graphics Corp.*[29] and *Princeton University Press v. Michigan Documents Service.*[30] They also recognize that the loss of royalties for reproduction in coursepacks fails the market effect test.

Classroom Guidelines

When the Copyright Act was being debated, the need to use copyrighted works in nonprofit education was recognized. An agreement was negotiated by representatives of publishers, authors, and educational associations and was presented to Congress. Called the Classroom Guidelines, the agreement covers classroom copying of books and periodicals in nonprofit educational institutions. These guidelines were published in the House Report that accompanied the act, and Congress recognized the agreement with approval.[31]

The guidelines detail conditions and tests that should be met when a teacher reproduces multiple copies of copyrighted works for classroom use. Although the guidelines indicate that they are minimum rather than maximum guidelines, many educational institutions apply them as if they were maximums. The guidelines also deal with single copying by teachers for their own use in teaching and research, but for purposes of this chapter, multiple copying is most important.[32] Teachers are permitted to make multiple copies of copyrighted works and distribute one copy to each student in the class if four tests are satisfied: brevity, spontaneity, cumulative effects, and copyright notice.[33]

The guidelines define brevity very specifically. For an article, brevity means an article of 2,500 words or less or an excerpt of 1,000 words or 10 percent, whichever is less, but a minimum of 500 words. The guidelines permit a poem to be copied if it is 250 words or less in length and is printed on two pages or less. If the copyrighted work is a graphic work, one meets the brevity test.[34] These word limitations are problematic for higher education. The American Association of University Professors and the Association of American Law Schools refused to endorse these guidelines because they found them too restrictive for colleges and universities.

Spontaneity means that the copying is done at the instigation of the individual teacher and is not directed by "higher authority." Further, the decision to reproduce the work must be made so late in the class term that there is no opportunity to obtain permission from the copyright owner.[35] The spontaneity requirement indicates that the purpose of the multiple copying for classroom use is for filling in, for presenting breaking news, or for using material of which the faculty member was previously unaware. In other words, it is not a coursepack.

There are several parts to cumulative effects. First, the copying may be done for only one course. If a teacher has multiple sections of a course, this is still one course. Second, the teacher may not repeat with respect to the same item from term to term. Such repeated copying cannot meet the spontaneity test for use of the same material in subsequent class terms. Third, only one article or other contribution from an author or two excerpts from an author during the class term, and no more than three from a periodical volume or other collective work may be reproduced and distributed to students. The fourth cumulative effect actually is the ultimate effect: No more than nine instances of such copying during the class term.[36]

There may be no charge to the students for the photocopies beyond the actual cost of copying. Further, each reproduced copy must contain a notice of copyright on the first page. Teachers are prohibited from using the guidelines to produce anthologies or to reproduce consumable works (such as standardized tests, answer sheets, or workbooks).[37]

Considerable criticism has been levied at the guidelines from the academic community. In fact, in its active opposition, the American Association of University Professors wrote to Congress encouraging rejection of the guidelines in any part of the legislative history.[38] Despite this opposition, the American Council of Education signed on to the guidelines, and many educational institutions have made them their own by including them in campus copyright policies.[39]

The guidelines have been litigated, but not in a case that deals specifically with reproduction and distribution of photocopies to students in a class by a teacher. The coursepack cases did discuss the guidelines with approval, however. In 1991, the Second Circuit discussed the guidelines in *Kinko's* because defendant Kinko's raised the guidelines as a defense to coursepack copying.[40] The court cited and discussed the guidelines with approval even though it found them inapplicable to Kinko's because it is a commercial copying service and the guidelines apply only to nonprofit educational institutions.[41] The Sixth Circuit sitting en banc also cited the guidelines with approval in *Michigan Documents Service*[42] when it reversed the earlier holding of its three-judge panel.[43] It discussed the guidelines and indicated that they applied to nonprofit educational institutions, which the copy center, Michigan Documents Service, was not. The majority classified Michigan Documents Service as a commercial copying service.[44] One dissenting judge stated that had the individual students made the copies or had the individual faculty members made multiple copies to distribute to the students, it would not have been infringement.[45]

Unfortunately, these cases appear to convert these safe harbor guidelines into maximum guidelines. They still have not been litigated with a proper defendant, however, i.e., a teacher who exceeds the guidelines or an educational institution that directs the copying by individual teachers. Nonetheless, courts have cited the guidelines with approval.

ALA Model Policy

After January 1, 1978, the effective date of the Copyright Act, libraries realized that nothing in either sections 107 or 108 dealt clearly with library reserves of photocopies of copyrighted works made to support individual classes, most often at the request of an individual faculty member. Many authorities argued in favor of a broad right for libraries to reproduce copies for reserve based on the Classroom Guidelines. Emeritus Professor of Law John C. Stedman of the University of Wisconsin-Madison stated that the provisions of the Classroom Guidelines should give considerable comfort to reserve collection managers. "[I]f it is permissible to make 'multiple copies for classroom use,' it would seem to follow logically that one could make a smaller number for use under the restrictive conditions that typically apply to a library reserve program."[46] He also stated that, normally, educational institutions would not photocopy entire works for reserve since it would be more economical to purchase the works; thus, the market effect of the copying would be minimal.[47] This contrasts with the *Texaco* holding, which found that the right to license to photocopy was an important right that caused negative market impact to the publishers when one in the for-profit sector avoids paying royalties.[48] Stedman did warn libraries to be careful to "avoid unreasonable and excessive photocopying."[49]

In 1982, because of questions from its members, the American Library Association issued its *Model Policy Concerning College and University Photocopying for Classroom, Research and Library Reserve Use*.[50] These guidelines are the least authoritative of any issued in connection with the Copyright Act in that they have no stamp of Congress whatsoever. Further, they do not represent negotiations between copyright holders and users; instead, they are merely the opinion of a library association, albeit the largest library organization. On the other hand, publishers apparently did not object to the ALA guidelines since they have instituted no litigation against libraries that adhere to them.[51]

The Model Policy guidelines begin with a statement that libraries may photocopy and place materials on reserve "in accordance with guidelines similar to those governing formal classroom distribution for face-to-face teaching. . . ."[52] This view was specifically rejected by the register of copyrights, however.[53] The policy goes on to state that the library reserve room functions as an extension to the classroom and that photocopying for reserve for convenience of the student simply reflects the individual student's right to copy materials for herself for class preparation, research, and the like, which is permitted under fair use. The ALA guidelines state that the Classroom Guidelines are in many ways inappropriate for colleges and universities because requirements such as brevity just cannot mean the same thing for higher education as they do for elementary schools. If the faculty member's request is for only one copy to be placed on reserve, then the library may copy an entire article, book chapter, or poem.[54]

The ALA Model Policy guidelines are divided into two parts. The first part restates some of the requirements from the Classroom Guidelines and states that, in general, materials photocopied for reserve should follow the "standard guidelines"; then the following restrictions are listed:

1. The distribution of the same materials does not occur every semester.
2. Only one copy is distributed for each student.
3. The material includes a copyright notice on the first page of the portion of the material photocopied.
4. The students are not assessed any fee beyond the actual cost of the photocopying.[55]

For requests to place multiple copies on reserve, the ALA Model Policy states that these guidelines should be met:

1. The amount of material should be reasonable in relation to the total amount of material assigned for one term of a course, taking into account the nature of the course, its subject matter, and level, 17 U.S.C. §107(1) and (3).
2. The number of copies should be reasonable in light of the number of students enrolled, the difficulty and timing of assignments, and the number of other courses that may assign the same material, 17 U.S.C. §107(1) and (3).
3. The material should contain a notice of copyright; see 17 U.S.C. §401.
4. The effect of photocopying the material should not be detrimental to the market for the work. (In general, the library should own at least one copy of the work.) 17 U.S.C. §107(4).[56]

Based on these statements, clearly library reserves are not meant to supersede the need for a textbook that students purchase or a coursepack for which permission is sought and royalties paid when requested. Materials photocopied for reserve may be assigned readings or optional; in either event, they are intended to complement a textbook or coursepack, not replace them. The second statement, concerning the number of copies of the reproduced material that are placed on reserve, leads to the conclusion that the library is better suited to make this decision than the faculty member. The effect of the photocopying should not be detrimental to the market for the work, and the only way to judge the effect on the market is to examine the parent work. If a faculty member requests that five chapters from a book be placed on reserve, the library needs to know how many chapters are in the book before it can make a determination about the market impact. In other words, five chapters from a six- or eight-chapter book is such a large portion that the faculty member should have had the students purchase the book. But if the book contains thirty-five chapters, five is such a small percentage that the professor likely would not have required students to purchase the book.

The portion of the ALA Model Policy regarding reserves that garners the most criticism is the statement from the Classroom Guidelines that "the distribution of the same photocopied material does not occur every semester." Many libraries believe this is too restrictive based on fair use, but others have incorporated the restriction into their reserve policies.

Many college and university libraries have developed reserve policies that comply with the reserve guidelines in the ALA Model Policy very carefully. Some libraries never go beyond the guidelines, while others are more expansive in their interpretation.[57] Too often, libraries have been the passive recipients of faculty requests for reserve materials. They have not made the necessary inquiries to determine whether a request satisfies the ALA Model Policy. Further, after the *Kinko's* decision, when faculty members determined that their coursepacks were too expensive if permission was sought and royalties paid, they began to put the material on reserve in the library for students to copy themselves. Libraries that accepted this material violated both the spirit and the provisions of the ALA Model Policy.

The huge majority of academic libraries either follow the ALA policy or have their own similar policies governing fair use. Nonetheless, publishers recently stated that they never agreed to the Model Policy, nor were they involved in its development. Additionally, they believe that reproducing entire articles is too much.[58]

ELECTRONIC RESERVE COLLECTIONS

It was only natural that libraries would turn to technology to solve a variety of problems caused by reserve collections. First, reserve collections occupy considerable space and are not easy to manage. Second, because the individual photocopied items are unbound pieces, they have to be placed in folders or other covers to prevent loss and to keep them with other reserve items for that course. Many libraries use file cabinets and file folders to maintain the materials. Others use pamphlet boxes or some other method of storing them on shelves. Third, because faculty members tend to reuse items, the library often has to photocopy the material again each semester as the copies are worn or marked on. Fourth, the items have to be checked out and back in as users retrieve and return them. Last, the library has to determine what to do with the items at the end of the semester. Some libraries return all items to the faculty member, while others retain them in the reserve collection. Still others hold onto the photocopies but do not permit them to circulate after the semester ends.

E-reserve systems are of several different types, but all include making a digital copy of an existing print work and then making the item available to students through a workstation; a system might also include links to digital materials licensed by the library. Some libraries permit only in-library use, but more currently or soon will permit access from anywhere through a network connection with authentication of users.

Benefits of Electronic Reserve Systems

Regardless of the decisions the library makes, the management and storage of the collection can be a problem. As libraries began to have computers and scanning technology available to them, it was inevitable that they would envision converting paper reserve collections to digital format. An electronic system solves many but not all of the problems inherent in a paper course reserve system. For example, an e-reserve system greatly reduces the space required to maintain the collection. It requires scanning only one time rather than repeated copying by the library; it reduces the necessity of finding storage means such as folders, pamphlet boxes, etc.; and staff members no longer have to check reserve items in and out.

Additionally, an electronic reserve system greatly increases the ways materials may be accessed. Not only can students search the items on the system in a variety of ways, but, since most e-reserve systems are established over the campus network, they can also retrieve materials both in the library (as with a paper reserve collection) and from their dormitory rooms, apartments, or wherever there is access to the network. With a paper collection, students may read the copy they check out or photocopy it for later reading. An electronic system adds an additional possibility. Not only may students read the item on the computer screen or print a copy, but they may also download it to a disk. They may then make notes right on the disk copy and rearrange the materials to facilitate their study.

An electronic system provides benefits for the library also. It can better manage the collection, provide enhanced bibliographic access to the materials on reserve, maintain permission records more accurately and efficiently, and store the items when the course is not being taught while still not permitting student access. It relieves demand for seating space within the library and generally delivers reserve items in more ways: onscreen viewing, downloading to a disk, or printing.

Copyright Concerns Unique to Electronic Reserves

Electronic reserve collections raise all of the copyright concerns that exist for a paper reserve collection and new ones as well. Many libraries determined that they would not attempt to obtain permission but would instead try to follow the reserve guidelines in the ALA Model Policy as a way to deal with copyright issues.[59] Others decided to seek permission for every item scanned into the e-reserve system.[60] A few libraries experimented with e-reserve systems but did not place anything in the system other than items on which the requesting faculty member held the copyright.[61]

Creating an e-reserve system raises unique copyright problems also. Clearly, an item is reproduced when it is scanned and placed into the system, but it is also reproduced whenever a student prints or downloads it. At least one recent case indicates that simply reading the item on the screen makes a copy of the copyrighted item.[62] Thus, an electronic system makes more copies of a work than are made in a photocopied collection. Further, publishers argue that the copy made is not a copy. but an original. In other words, there is no degradation of the quality of the copy when it is reproduced either through printing or downloading to disk as currently occurs when a photocopy is further reproduced.[63] On the other hand, when the use is made for nonprofit educational purposes, it may be a fair use.

Because of the ease of further reproduction once an item is digitized, publishers fear uncontrolled reproduction. They believe students are likely to upload reserve items onto electronic discussion lists and, "with a few keystrokes, transmit the work to 100,000 people."[64] This is not possible with paper reserve systems because the item is not in digital format. While it is not possible to ensure absolutely that such uncontrolled distribution will not occur, the library can take steps to prevent this. For example, each copyrighted item included in the e-reserve system should display the notice of copyright along with an additional statement to the effect that no further electronic distribution of the copyrighted work is permitted.

Another possible copyright problem of an e-reserve system that is accessed in a public area may also infringe the display right of copyright owners. It is only the right of public display that is an exclusive right of the owner. A public display is defined as one that occurs in a place that is open to the public or where a substantial number of persons outside the normal circle of family and friends are gathered.[65] Thus, displaying a digital copy on a computer screen in a public area of the library may be a public display. On the other hand, how likely is it that a group of students or members of the public are going to be so interested in a reserve item that they flock to a computer workstation in a public area of the library to view a display of an item on reserve? Not very!

Copyright holders are also concerned that access to and use of the material will increase, which will reduce the sales of the parent volume or royalties they would otherwise receive for photocopying. This concern has two aspects. One is that ease of access to the electronic system will increase the number of people who use the reproduction of the copyrighted work. This certainly could be the case if the library simply makes all reserve items available over the campus network because individuals not enrolled in the course can access the material. If users from outside the university also have access, the problem is exacerbated. The library can ensure that this does not occur by restricting access to the materials reproduced in the system to students, faculty, and staff of the institution or to students who are enrolled in that course. The other aspect is that the electronic system can easily provide increased bibliographic access points if individual articles and chapters are cataloged and entered into an online catalog. This concern can also be alleviated by simply avoiding cataloging to the article-specific level unless all journals are so cataloged in the library. In other words, bibliographic entry points should be under the name of the faculty member and the number or name of the course.

When a library obtains a work in digital format (as opposed to converting a paper copy to digital format only), the license agreement that accompanies the work will control whether portions of the work can be included in an e-reserve system. While there will still be fair use, the library exemption contains a statement that nothing "affects any contractual obligations assumed at any time by the library or archives when it obtained a copy or phonorecord of a work in its collection."[66] So, if the license prohibits reproduction of materials for reserve, the license is binding. Linking to the digital work should not be a problem unless the license agreement prohibits such links, and libraries should negotiate such licenses to enable linking from the e-reserve system to the licensed digital work.

ELECTRONIC RESERVE GUIDELINES

When the Information Infrastructure Task Force's report, *Intellectual Property and the National Information Infrastructure*, called for a Conference on Fair Use (CONFU) to determine whether it was possible to develop guidelines for the fair use of copyrighted works in the digital environment, many librarians assumed that electronic reserves would be one of these issues.[67] Beginning in October 1994, CONFU met regularly and worked on a series of guidelines, among them e-reserves. The proposed Electronic Reserve Guidelines were completed by a small working group. They recognized that materials included in an e-reserve system should constitute an ad hoc or supplemental source for students and should not take the place of a textbook, coursepack, or other materials.[68]

Despite initial support for the Electronic Reserve Guidelines, neither most library associations nor the Association of American Publishers (AAP) endorsed them, and they were not included in the final report of CONFU.[69] A number of organizations, including the American Council of Learned Societies, the American Association of Law

Libraries, Special Libraries Association, and the Association of American University Presses, did endorse the guidelines, however. The library associations that did not endorse them stated that they were too restrictive on libraries. The Association of American Publishers said the guidelines went far beyond fair use since they permitted reproduction of entire articles and chapters rather than small portions.[70] One could posit that the draft guidelines struck the appropriate balance, since both sides found them going too far in the other's direction.

The Guidelines

The guidelines attempt to differentiate between the primary materials assigned for a course and the complementary or supplementary readings of copyrighted articles and chapters that might be found in a typical reserve collection. They equate digitizing the materials with placing them in a collection of photocopies for course reserves and thus permit reproduction of entire journal articles and book chapters. As Peter Grenquist, executive director of the Association of American University Presses, stated, "There are costs on both sides. Publishers will have to bear some of the costs and so will libraries."[71] Publishers may receive reduced royalties because of this one-term use without permission, but libraries bear the cost of managing the system, implementing it, and explaining certain restrictions.

The proposed guidelines detail several requirements that should alleviate some of the concerns of copyright owners. These limitations include: (a) use of an article or chapter in an e-reserve system for only one term without obtaining permission from the copyright holder, (b) restricting access to the e-reserve materials to students enrolled in the course, (c) including admonishments that no further distribution of the material is permitted, and (d) no more detailed bibliographic access to the material than is provided for other journal articles.

One-Time Use

The ALA Model Policy indicates that photocopies should be placed on reserve for only one semester. The proposed Electronic Reserve Guidelines contain the same limitation. Because a digital copy of a work is, in effect, an original, and because each copy printed from the digital copy also is an original, the one-time-use limitation attempts to balance the rights of the copyright holder with the rights of the nonprofit educational user. It recognizes that repeated use likely is beyond what can be considered a fair use. Librarians must recognize that a digital copy may be different from a photocopy and for this reason one-time use is a fair restriction. The AAP believes that even one-time use is not a fair use, however.[72]

Restricting Access to Enrolled Students

Because there is a possibility of abuse, making e-reserve course materials available only to students enrolled in the course goes a long way to reduce concerns of copyright holders. While the likelihood that others outside of the course might be interested in reading the materials for the course reserve is slight, this limitation is one of the costs that the library or school should bear.

Student access can be restricted in a variety of ways with varying technological methods. Each institution can select its own method for verifying that the student who seeks access to the material is enrolled in the course. The library can control this verification method entirely and needs little sophistication to do so. One of the simplest methods would be to assign each course an access number that is distributed only to students in the course. At the other end of the spectrum would be a system that automatically verifies course enrollment when a student enters his or her PIN number. Some institutions already have the technology to implement such systems.

Statement Prohibiting Further Distribution

The proposed Electronic Reserve Guidelines dictate that each copyrighted item in the digital system should contain notice of copyright. This complies with the Classroom Guidelines and with the ALA Model Policy. Because of the fairly low level of retrieval of reserve materials generally, the likelihood that students will upload the work onto an electronic discussion list seems remote. However, many students do not recognize that the copyright notice means works should not be transmitted to others through an electronic discussion list; thus, a statement to the effect that "further electronic transmission or distribution of this work is prohibited" alerts them that such transmission is considered multiple reproduction of the copyrighted work, which is seldom held a fair use. If such a statement appears along with the copyright notice, the student is alerted that further transmission or copying is also an infringement of copyright. This is another of the costs that the institution should bear, and it is not burdensome.

Bibliographic Access

The problem with bibliographic access was detailed above. The proposed Electronic Reserve Guidelines dictate that libraries should not provide bibliographic access at any greater level of detail than is done for other journal articles and book chapters. Access should be limited to course name, course number, and name of the faculty member. This reduces the likelihood that students not enrolled in the course will seek access to the materials.

Other Issues

Publishers and librarians have disagreed quite vigorously over electronic reserves. To date, however, there has been no litigation nor even a reported cease and desist letter over electronic reserves. Likewise, there has been no litigation over the ALA Model Policy and, in fact, little comment about the policy from the publishing community despite the fact that these were not negotiated guidelines.[73] This began to change when libraries started implementing electronic reserve systems. Libraries have found it difficult to obtain permission from publishers to include their works in an electronic reserve system, even when they are willing to pay royalties. Other publishers charge such high royalties that they in effect deny permission for use. Some do not respond to library requests at all. The Copyright Clearance Center has helped somewhat, but it, too, is restricted by what copyright holders are willing to license them to do.

The Copyright Clearance Center (CCC), a nonprofit corporation organized to collect royalties for use that exceeds fair-use photocopying, has created the electronic commerce content service (ECCS) to handle royalties for digital copying for electronic reserves and for providing digital course materials to distance education students.[74] If the proposed Electronic Reserve Guidelines are followed, then there may be more permissions sought and royalties paid than would otherwise occur. Those guidelines exempt the first term use of the item in the reserve collection in accordance with the Classroom Guidelines but suggest that permission be sought for subsequent uses. Thus, the CCC's system for reserves will make it considerably easier for both libraries and copyright holders.

One benefit of the ECCS is that materials cleared through the service may be accessed by faculty and students as electronic coursepacks, e-reserves, or distance learning. ECCS bills itself as one-stop shopping for copyright permissions for e-reserves, and many publications are more or less precleared through the CCC's blanket permissions with some publishers. The CCC eliminated its membership annual registration fees in 1999, but it still charges a service fee ranging from $2.50 to $6.50 per item based on the formula of fifteen cents per page and the number of students. This fee is in addition to any royalty fees established by publishers. Thus, the service fee simply covers CCC costs.[75] Royalty fees vary considerably. Online registration and permission requests speed permission through the CCC, but it still takes four to six weeks on average.

The CCC asks that works cleared through the ECCS contain the following statement in addition to the copyrighted notice: "Reproduced with the permission of [copyright holder] via the Copyright Clearance Center." Another benefit of the online system is that it is possible to check on the status of requests electronically.[76]

Users complain that having to request permission in each subsequent term that the work is used is cumbersome and seems unnecessary. The CCC, however, states that it is bound by contract to contact the copyright holder for each term's use. Also, since individual publishers set their own per page or per article royalty, fees may change from semester to semester.[77]

Music libraries in educational institutions have long housed reserve collections consisting of audiotapes reproduced from sound recordings. Libraries produced tapes from library copies of sound recordings to support classroom instruction at the request of individual instructors. Students then were assigned to come into the music library to listen to the copy of the recording. Often, the library made multiple copies of the tapes to meet the needs of the class. Whether this was infringement under the statute or the existing ALA Model Policy is problematic, but it was never litigated. The Guidelines on the Educational Use of Music certainly do not mention this broad practice. Their only mention of reproducing sound recordings is the statement that copies of small portions of sound recordings could be made for the purpose of constructing aural exercises.[78] Today, many of these music libraries are using streaming audio to provide the same access that the tapes provided. Does streaming audio make a copy of multiple copies of works? If so, does it constitute copyright infringement? The Music Library Association has taken the official position that it does not, since students are permitted only to listen to the work, but not to make copies.[79] Copyright holders likely feel that this is infringement of their reproduction and perhaps even performance rights, but there has been no litigation over the issue.

CONCLUSION

The availability of digital technology presents an excellent opportunity for both libraries and copyright holders to reexamine their policies and determine how reserve collections can take advantage of this new technology while still complying with copyright law. The law is focused not on benefiting the owners of copyrights, but on the public good. The law exists to "promote the progress of science and the useful arts,"[80] not to ensure economic rewards to authors and publishers.[81] Promotion of learning is thus a constitutional purpose, and one way it is facilitated is through nonprofit educational uses of copyrighted works. Reproducing works for library reserves is such a use. Reserve collections help ensure that materials are available in the library to support courses taught in the institution. E-reserve collections simply apply new technology to old reserve collections. Because of the differences in digital works and photocopies, however, there must be some controls on libraries' abilities to digitize works and make them available.

The AAP's rejection of the proposed CONFU Electronic Reserve Guidelines is perhaps understandable, but university presses did not sign on to the guidelines either. University presses comprise about 18 percent of the membership of the AAP, and materials published by university presses make up a large portion of the materials reproduced for reserve collections. Publishers may have assumed that libraries would not place their materials into e-reserve collections if the AAP objected to the guidelines; this may be accurate. It may also mean that the publishers' materials are no longer used for course reserves and the publisher loses too, along with the students who would have been exposed to the ideas contained in the works, but now will not. Or it could mean that libraries simply ignore copyright concerns.

Most librarians are law-abiding citizens who want to comply with the copyright law. Unrealistic restrictions, outright denial of use for e-reserves, and unreasonable royalty fees on the part of publishers may discourage compliance. A library may argue that fair use permits the inclusion of works to support courses in a nonprofit educational institution through a password-protected e-reserve system. Further, the statute itself provides a good-faith defense for library employees for those who are truly acting in good faith.[82]

Eleventh Amendment immunity may also protect state-supported institutions. The U.S. Supreme Court recently ruled that a state agency could not be sued for damages in a patent case.[83] Individuals, however, still could be sued for damages, and institutions could be sued for an injunction. This may mean that there is little risk to libraries in state-supported institutions for any copyright infringement that might occur with electronic reserves.

One solution many faculty members may seek is to avoid library electronic reserves and put materials directly on a faculty or course home page.[84] The same considerations likely exist for course web pages, and a faculty member may not only be personally liable for copyright infringement, but may also create liability for the institution.[85]

It is unlikely that copyright considerations will kill e-reserve collections. Libraries as well as publishers must be permitted to use technology to serve their users. Unrealistic restrictions on the part of publishers may mean that more libraries simply ignore the law and claim that any use, even repeated use, for e-reserves is a fair use. In order to challenge this, publishers would be forced to litigate. Eleventh Amendment immunity provides considerable protection for state-supported institutions. Fair, easy, fast, and cost-effective licensing is the answer.

NOTES

1. See American Library Association, *Model Policy Concerning College and University Photocopying for Classroom, Research, and Library Reserve Use* (Chicago: ALA, 1982), reprinted in 43 *College and Research Libraries News* (1982): 127 (hereinafter ALA Model Policy).

2. *Library Journal* 3 (1878): 271.

3. Charles Harvey Brown, *Circulation Work in College and University Libraries* 19 (1933), citing 2 *Library Notes* (1887): 216.

4. Ibid., 80. Few librarians have noted much decline in reserve collections; in fact, quite the opposite over the past quarter century.

5. Ibid., 84.

6. Ibid., 88.

7. Ibid., 89.

8. Ibid., 162.

9. Statements of Mary Jackson, Association of Research Libraries, at the Conference on Fair Use, Washington, D.C., October 25, 1995.

10. National Research Council Staff, *The Digital Dilemma: The Future of Intellectual Property in the Information Infrastructure* (Washington, D.C.: National Academy Press, 2000), 132–36.

11. Theodore W. Koch, "A Symposium on the Reserve Book System," in *College and University Library Service: Trends, Standards, Appraisal, Problems* (Chicago: American Library Association, 1938), 73, 74.

12. 17 U.S.C. §109(a) (1994). In several European countries, there is a public lending right that generates royalties for copyright holders. The United States has not enacted such a provision, nor is it likely to do so. For a discussion of the public lending right abroad, see Laura N. Gasaway and Sarah K. Wiant, *Libraries and Copyright: A Guide to Copyright Law in the Nineties* (Washington, D.C.: Special Libraries Association, 1994), 199–216.

13. 17 U.S.C. §§101–1332.

14. Ibid., §106.

15. Ibid., §107.

16. Ibid.

17. Some argue that fair use is a right as opposed to solely a defense; the dispute is discussed in *The Digital Dilemma,* supra, note 10, at 206.

18. Paul Goldstein, *Copyright Set,* 2d ed. (New York: Aspen Law & Business, 1996) (hereinafter Goldstein).

19. *American Geophysical Union v. Texaco, Inc.,* 60 F.3d 913, 923 (2d Cir. 1994).

20. Senate Report No. 976, 93d Cong. (1974), reprinted in 13 *Omnibus Copyright Revision Legislative History* 117 (1977) (hereinafter Senate Report).

21. *American Geophysical Union v. Texaco,* 925.

22. Senate Report, supra, note 20.

23. *American Geophysical Union v. Texaco,* 926.

24. See *Harper & Row, Inc. v. The Nation Enterprises,* 471 U.S. 539, 566 (1985) for a case in which the qualitative part of this factor was critical to the holding that the use was not a fair one.

25. Ibid.

26. *Acuff-Rose v. Campbell,* 510 U.S. 569 (1994), 578.

27. *American Geophysical Union v. Texaco*, 931.

28. Ibid., 931–32.

29. *Basic Books, Inc. v. Kinko's Graphics Corp.*, 758 F. Supp. 1522. (S.D.N.Y. 1991).

30. *Princeton University Press v. Michigan Documents Service*, 99 F.3d 1381 (6th Cir. 1996).

31. House Report No. 1467, 94th Cong. (1976), reprinted in *Omnibus Copyright Law Revision Legislation* 68–71 (1977) (hereinafter House Report).

32. Ibid., 68.

33. Ibid., 68–69.

34. Ibid.

35. Ibid., 69.

36. Ibid.

37. Ibid., 69–70.

38. See John C. Stedman, "The New Copyright Law: Photocopying for Educational Use," 63 *AAUP Bulletin*, February 1977, 5, 15.

39. Kenneth D. Crews, *Copyright, Fair Use, and the Challenges for Universities: Promoting the Progress of Higher Education* (Chicago: University of Chicago Press, 1993), 68 (hereinafter Crews).

40. *Basic Books, Inc. v. Kinko's Graphics Corp.*, 758 F. Supp. 1522 (2d Cir. 1992).

41. Ibid., 1535–37.

42. *Princeton University Press v. Michigan Documents Service*, supra, note 30.

43. 74 F.3d 1528 (6th Cir. 1996).

44. *Princeton University Press v. Michigan Documents Service*, 1390–91.

45. Ibid., 1393–94 (Martin, J., dissenting).

46. John C. Stedman, "Academic Library Reserves, Photocopying and the Copyright Law," *College and Research Library News* 39 (1978): 263, 265 (hereinafter Stedman).

47. Ibid.

48. *American Geophysical Union v. Texaco*, 931.

49. Stedman, supra, note 46, 267.

50. ALA Model Policy, supra, note 1.

51. See Gasaway, supra, note 12, 148–49.

52. ALA Model Policy, supra, note 1, 127.

53. James S. Heller, *Copyright Handbook* (Chicago: American Association of Law Libraries, 1984), 28–29.

54. ALA Model Policy, supra, note 1, 129.

55. Ibid., 129.

56. Ibid.

57. Crews, supra, note 39, 87–88.

58. The statements were made by publishers' representatives, including Carol Risher of the Association of American Publishers and Harriet Goldberg of Simon & Schuster, at various sessions of the Conference on Fair Use, Washington, D.C., October 1994–November 1996.

59. Duke University Library took this approach when it initiated its electronic reserve system in 1992.

60. One of the first electronic reserve systems implemented was at San Diego State University (SDSU), which seeks permission and pays royalties if requested for each item in the system. For an article that describes the SDSU system, see Richard J. Goodram, "The E-RBR: Confirming the Technology and Exploring the Law of Electronic Reserves: Two Generations of the Digital Library System at the SDSU Library," 22 *Journal of Academic Librarianship* 118 (1996).

61. The University of Pittsburgh Library originally chose this alternative as it began to adopt electronic reserves and included course syllabi, faculty developed problem sets, and the like.

62. See *MAI Systems Corp. v. Peak Computer, Inc.,* 991 F.2d 511 (9th Cir. 1993). Many scholars disagree with this holding and believe that transitory copies do not equate with a true reproduction of a copyrighted work. That copy is viewed as incidental to the use.

63. Few users would find the perfect copy argument persuasive with traditional works in reserve collections such as articles, book chapters, and the like. It is a stronger argument, however, for audiovisual and musical works.

64. Risher, Association of American Publishers, statement at the Conference on Fair Use, Washington, D.C., January 4, 1995.

65. 17 U.S.C. §101 (1994).

66. Ibid., §108(f)(4).

67. United States Information Infrastructure Task Force, *Intellectual Property and the National Information Infrastructure: Report of the Working Group on Intellectual Property Rights,* Bruce A. Lehman, chair (Washington, D.C.: U.S. Patent and Trademark Office, 1995), 83–84. Available at www.uspto.gov/web/offices/com/doc/ipnii/index.html.

68. Although never adopted by CONFU, the 1996 draft electronic reserve guidelines are available on several web sites. See, for example, www.utsystem.edu/ogc/intellectualproperty/rsvrguid.htm and www.cc.columbia.edu/~rosedale/guidelines.html. They are also reprinted in *Growing Pains: Adapting Copyright for Libraries, Education, and Society,* ed. Laura Gasaway (Littleton, Colo.: Fred Rothman, 1997), 499.

69. AAP statement on e-reserves presented at Conference on Fair Use, Washington, D.C., May 26, 1996 (hereinafter AAP Statement).

70. Ibid.
71. Statement of Peter Grenquist at the Conference on Fair Use, Washington, D.C., May 30, 1996.
72. AAP Statement, supra, note 69.
73. During the CONFU process, publishers referred to the fact that these were not negotiated guidelines and that they had never agreed to them. On the other hand, publishers have not filed suit against a library for photocopying materials for its reserve collection. One might query whether this indicates acquiescence to the practice or whether it was viewed as so unimportant that litigation was unnecessary.
74. The CCC's electronic course content service is described at www. copyright.com/Services/ECCS.html.
75. Ibid.
76. Ibid.
77. Ibid.
78. House Report, supra, note 31, at 70–71. These guidelines are similar to the classroom guidelines in that they were negotiated and were published in the legislative history that accompanied the Copyright Act.
79. See Music Library Association, Statement on the Digital Transmission of Electronic Reserves. www.musiclibraryassoc.org/Copyright/ereserves.htm.
80. U.S. Constitution, art. I, sec. 8, cl. 8.
81. *Feist Publications v. Rural Telephone Service*, 499 U.S. 340, 349 (1991).
82. 17 U.S.C. §504(c)(2) (1994).
83. *College Savings Bank v. Florida Prepaid Post Secondary Education Expense Board*, 527 U.S. 627 (1999). Although outside the scope of this paper there is every indication that this patent case, which held that state institutions enjoy immunity from suit for patent infringement, may also be applicable to copyright.
84. For an excellent discussion of these issues, see Steven J. Melamut, "Pursuing Fair Use, Law Libraries and Electronic Reserves," *Law Library Journal* 92 (2000): 157.
85. Online service provider liability was added to the Copyright Act in 1998. See 17 U.S.C. §512, Limitations on Liability Relating to Material Online. This section took effect on October 28, 1998, pursuant to §203 of the act, P.L. 105–304, which appears as a note to this section.

8

Electronic Reserves and the Digital Library

PASCAL V. CALARCO

This chapter will explore the relationship between electronic reserves and digital libraries. Topics include the evolution and definition of digital libraries, early electronic reserve projects within digital libraries, staffing models for digital library teams in academic libraries, digital library infrastructure, and developing trends. A case study of bootstrapping legacy integrated library systems as a digital library project concludes the discussion.

DIGITAL LIBRARY AND THE PROBLEM OF DEFINITION

The connection between electronic reserves and digital libraries is not immediately obvious. To many, they seem to be incongruous in many respects. Part of this disconnect is definitional; the term *digital library* means something different to the various communities involved in its research, development, deployment, and maintenance.[1] To the computer science community involved in research and development, a digital library is a fairly well-defined set of systems engineering activities and challenges involved with advanced information storage and retrieval in the distributed heterogeneous network environment. To librarians, a digital library is collections-oriented or services-oriented, providing a broad array of integrated library systems technologies and digitized collections organized to make unique and heavily used resources available in an organized, usable, user-oriented, Web-based environment. In the popular media, the Internet is often referred to as a digital library, where all of the world's information can be found for free, albeit in a somewhat chaotic, fluid manner.[2]

In contrast, *electronic reserves* refers to a well-understood, very specific set of services and activities in development and evolution for nearly ten years. However, even within the academic library community, the differences between electronic reserves and digital libraries are marked. In terms of collection retention, e-reserves are ephemeral, while digital library collections are often digitized special collections for the longer term where archival standards and issues are paramount. In terms of quality, e-reserves are digitized to minimize file size, perhaps at the expense of quality, whereas items stored in a digital library often push the upper limits of resolution, color depth, and storage requirements. This chapter will tackle some of these differences and similarities and will examine trends that are bringing e-reserves and the digital library toward an integrated whole.

Digital Library Defined: Historical Evolution

The definition of a digital library is still evolving. Although a number of authors have written on the subject, a digital library still means different things to different communities.[3] It would be instructive to look at the evolution of the term from its earliest use to the present day.

The earliest occurrences of "digital library" date to the mid-1980s in the electronics and electrical engineering literature.[4] The earliest use of the term in the indexed literature within a library science context can be attributed to Clifford Lynch, in his 1991 article about electronic futures in academic libraries.[5] During this period before the popularization of the World Wide Web (1991–1993), digital library was used in this fairly generic context to refer to the future of electronic library collections. Several other terms are found in the literature of the time, including "electronic library," "virtual library," and "library without walls." All of these terms were used in a fairly fluid continuum of meaning.[6]

With the advent of the National Information Infrastructure of the Clinton-Gore administration in the early 1990s and National Science Foundation funding beginning in 1994, digital library became a much more narrowly focused term. The NSF-funded projects were heavily oriented towards systems engineering and computer science approaches to basic research problems in large-scale multimedia database construction and information retrieval.[7] To some in the library community, it seemed that the purpose and scope of digital libraries were being co-opted by the computer science and engineering communities. In parallel developments, academic libraries had begun digitization projects, most of which initially focused on primary source material in special collections and archives departments.

Also during this time, efforts in developing and detailing best practices for digitization, organization, and description emerged from the selective academic library community involved in the U.S.-based Digital Library Federation. Library-based digital library researchers and librarians in the academic library community began to advance definitions of their own. The Digital Library Federation offered this definition:

> Digital libraries are organizations that provide the resources, including the specialized staff, to select, structure, offer intellectual access to, interpret, distribute, preserve the integrity of, and ensure the persistence over time of collections of digital works so that they are readily and economically available for use by a defined community or set of communities.[8]

A similar broad definition of the elements for a digital library was offered by another Council on Library Information Resources publication in 1994, here sponsored by the Association of College and Research Libraries:

> The digital library is not a single entity.
>
> The digital library requires technology to link the resources of many.
>
> The linkages between the many digital libraries and information services are transparent to end users.
>
> Universal access to digital libraries and information services is a goal.
>
> Digital library collections are not limited to document surrogates; they extend to digital artifacts that cannot be represented or distributed in printed form.[9]

These academic library definitions offer a much broader interpretation of digital libraries than mere technology. They also encompass digital library services and collections, two items not always explicitly included in digital library research with a computer science focus.

EARLY ELECTRONIC RESERVE PROJECTS IN DIGITAL LIBRARIES

Electronic reserve applications within larger digital library efforts were fairly rare in the early to mid-1990s. The early electronic reserve projects that were part of a larger digital library infrastructure tended to be demonstration projects using new technology platforms that did not necessarily mature into production offerings. Two examples of early electronic reserve projects that successfully moved to production systems are the VARIATIONS Project at Indiana University and the MERIT Project at the Marist College Library.

The VARIATIONS Project: Sound Recording Reserves with Digitized Scores

The VARIATIONS Project is a continuing digital library project at the Indiana University William and Gayle Cook Music Library.[10] It was conceived in 1990 by Michael Burroughs and David Fenske, music library director at that time, to investigate applications of new technologies into the music curricula, and it evolved to a music research and instruction focus.[11] The project uses several emerging technologies centered around the IBM VideoCharger and Digital Library products to digitize, provide access to, and archive music performances and their accompanying scores. As of mid-1999, the collection had more than 5,000 works, with 75 hours of music added each week.[12]

The VARIATIONS Project features a number of important linkages to other library systems that are standard in electronic reserve systems today. The bibliographic MARC record stores the location of the online digital sound recording in the MARC 856 field, a standard that has been in place for a number of years now. Indiana also employs the Z39.50 standard for linking distributed databases to tie the NOTIS LMS and web interface together, as illustrated in figure 1.

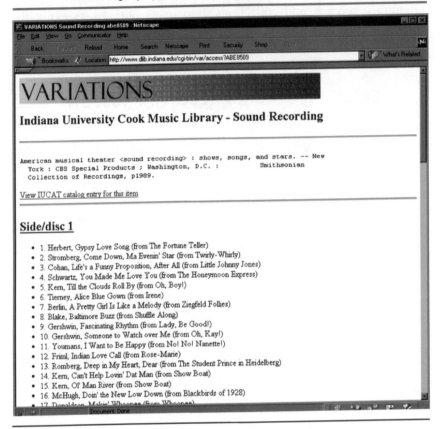

The project also integrates a digitized sheet music collection for some of the recordings, as shown in figure 2. The student thus has access to the score as well as recordings performed of the same music. An experimental prototype of an integrated player has also been developed at Indiana, allowing the pages to advance synchronously with the recording. As Indiana migrates from NOTIS LMS to an EpyxTech Horizon system in 2001, the system will evolve and integrate all of these features more fully.

FIGURE 2 **Digitized score pages with links to catalog bibliographic record**

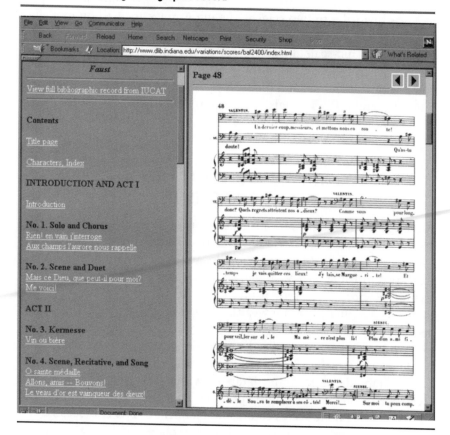

The MERIT Project at Marist College

The MERIT Project at Marist College in Poughkeepsie, New York, is another example of an early use of electronic reserves within a larger formal digital library project. This project, a four-year collaboration between Marist and IBM that began in 1996, not only seeks to develop infrastructure for course reserves, but also to serve as a central resource for digital content throughout the college. Marist defined the aim of this digital library in a community context: "to build a centralized repository of large networked databases containing digitized content in various formats with a single point of entry available anywhere on campus."[13]

The Marist implementation of the IBM Digital Library product was initially developed in a mainframe System/390 environment. The project was divided into two stages. The initial stage focused on modeling an electronic reserve room as a foundation technology; the second phase built a full-scale digital library to support the curriculum across the college and serve as a central repository for digitized content. The components in this second phase were ambitiously diverse: electronic journals, archival materials, photographic images, CD-ROM databases, and media files.

BOOTSTRAPPING LEGACY SYSTEMS FOR E-RESERVES

Although many of the current generation of integrated online library systems (IOLS) now include features that enable linkages to external collections locally held or at remote locations on the Internet, libraries that are still using legacy systems can bootstrap them for web-based, secured electronic reserves using a number of relatively easy-to-use tools. At Virginia Commonwealth University (VCU), librarians have been employing the latest generation of web application development tools to enable web-based electronic reserves with their existing legacy NOTIS LMS (see fig. 3). As of NOTIS LMS version 7.0, the course reserves module, a separate database within the system, is not web accessible through the WebPAC product, which is the front end for the OPAC (online public access catalog) component of NOTIS. Because the NOTIS system at VCU is expected to be replaced within two years, a web-enabling option requiring great time or expense was not possible. VCU conducted a pilot project during 1999–2000 that used customized versions of the FreeReserves and Open Source Course Reserves, which were programming using a variety of open source tools (Perl, MySQL, and PHP most significantly).

After assessing the feature set and maintenance issues with these tools, the VCU Libraries chose to work with a rapid development tool and application environment, Allaire ColdFusion, to enable web access to the NOTIS course reserve module (see fig. 4).[14] ColdFusion is a server-side scripting environment that allows very rapid development time (the conversion of the OSCR code from Perl and PHP to Cold-Fusion took about 30 hours programming time, including modification

FIGURE 3 Opening screen of the Virginia Commonwealth University Libraries' electronic reserves

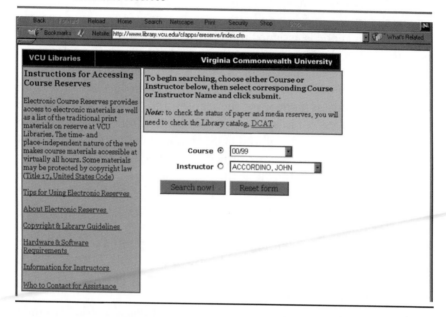

FIGURE 4 ColdFusion-generated course reserve results screen with links to full text

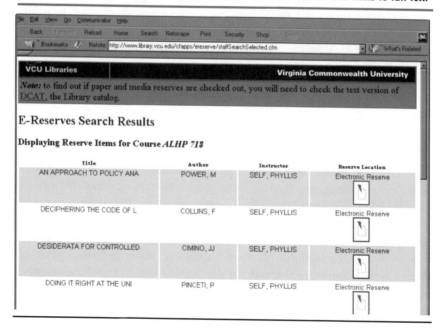

to the HTML presentation). The NOTIS course reserve module is used as it normally has been, with unlinked item records created on the staff side of the system. Additionally, for the electronic items, an electronic access location code is assigned to the item record, along with an accession number in the Notes field of the record. The reserve readings are then scanned and digitized using Adobe Acrobat and saved directly to a directory on an NT web server that is also running the ColdFusion server. The accession number for the reading and filename are stored in a Microsoft Access table at the time of digitization. Automated SAS Report extracts of the full NOTIS course reserve database to a Microsoft Access table are performed twice per week, and users are able to browse records for all of the items on reserve—print, audiovisual materials, and electronic—over the Web. The only major loss of functionality with this system is that the availability status of the print and audiovisual items in the NOTIS system can't be determined in the web-based system. ColdFusion also provides support for Java and a number of enterprise-level standards, including CORBA, RMI, JavaBeans, and others, so that the system can grow beyond server-side scripting when it needs to.

Although VCU Libraries are using ColdFusion for dynamic database-driven web development in other areas, they expect to retire the electronic reserves ColdFusion back end when they move to a latest-generation IOLS in about two years. ColdFusion has been a quick and relatively easy way for VCU to bridge legacy systems and the latest web technologies for the short term.

THE FUTURE OF ELECTRONIC RESERVES AND DIGITAL LIBRARIES

The past five years have seen remarkable change in the technology libraries are using to provide electronic reserves. Libraries initially employed gopher, then specialized first-generation digital library products, the World Wide Web, and finally we are seeing a move back to the library integrated online system as library system vendors release products that integrate digital library functions. Although the pace of change remains very rapid, several developing trends can be discerned with regards to how electronic reserves and digital libraries relate to one another.

Emerging Trends

Digital library teams develop and support electronic reserve services

Increasingly, digital library teams specializing in new technology development are being formed in academic libraries. These teams are usually organizationally separate from the traditional automation department, which handles the operational areas within academic libraries such as IOLS support and maintenance, local area networking and support, and desktop installation, support, and maintenance. Two good examples of this organization include North Carolina State University's digital library initiatives department and Indiana University's digital library team.[15,16] These teams are often formed by reorganizing existing technically savvy staff from public service units, systems departments, and other units across the library into a new department. One of the first projects these teams work on is developing or implementing an open-source, homegrown, or commercial electronic reserves system. Electronic reserves is a highly visible project that a digital library team can develop in collaboration with circulation staff, one that offers a practical service that balances out some of the more experimental and research-oriented activities of digital library teams.

The library IOLS becomes the primary digital library infrastructure

The latest generation of library systems by companies such as ExLibris, SIRSI, Innovative Interfaces, VTLS, and Endeavor Systems all feature support and extensibility for digital library collections. While the legacy mainframe-based library systems of the 1970s through the early 1990s were the majority systems in use, libraries had to turn to specialized external systems such as the IBM Digital Library, OCLC SiteSearch/SiteBuilder, and other relational database products to provide the infrastructure for digital library collections. Now, as libraries migrate to the latest generation of systems providing this functionality, we will increasingly see the central digital library system be the library IOLS.

Electronic reserves are integrated into MyLibrary personalized library portals

The web "portal" phenomenon in the form of MyLibrary has come to academic libraries within the last two years, and the most advanced of these systems are integrating not only links to electronic resources and digital collections, but also electronic services such as remote reference, document delivery, and electronic reserves as well. NCSU's MyLibrary already provides personalized links to reserve courses for students, and many other MyLibrary projects across the nation are following suit.[17] The sheer amount of electronic information available to today's student and researcher is driving these personalization services, as people attempt to manage the deluge of information available to them.

CONCLUSION

This chapter has sought to provide some background to a still-evolving topic in academic librarianship: digital libraries and electronic reserves. It examined the challenges in defining digital libraries; various definitions from systems-centric and services- or collections-centric communities; two early electronic reserve projects that laid the foundations for integrating today's services into larger digital library efforts; and one institution's strategy in bootstrapping legacy library systems to enable web-based electronic reserves. The discussion concluded with a look ahead to developing trends in integrating digital libraries and electronic reserves in a networked environment.

NOTES

1. C. L. Borgman, "What Are Digital Libraries? Competing Visions," *Information Processing & Management* 35, no. 2 (1999): 227–43.

2. See, for example, Rajiv Chandrasekaran, "Seeing the Sites on a Custom Tour; New Internet Search Tool Takes Selective Approach," *Washington Post,* Sept. 4, 1997, E01.

   "For more than a year, a team of computer industry entrepreneurs has been using a roomful of computers to copy every World Wide Web page they can find. Their massive digital library originally was viewed as a quixotic venture to assemble an Internet time capsule of the global computer network's early days. But the electronic librarians appear to have found a more immediate—and potentially profitable—use for their 2 trillion-character pile of data: a new and precise way for ordinary computer users to navigate the sprawling Web."

3. See Sarah B. Watstein, Pascal V. Calarco, and James S. Ghaphery, "Digital Library: Keywords," *Reference Services Review* 27, no. 4 (1999): 344–52; K. Klemperer and S. Chapman, "Digital Libraries: A Selected Resource Guide," *Information Technology & Libraries* 16, no. 3 (1997); Susan Davis Herring, "Journal Literature on Digital Libraries: Publishing and Indexing Patterns, 1992–1997," *College & Research Libraries* 161, no. 1 (2000): 39–44.

4. See the following examples: "The Digital Studio," *Middle East Electronics* 8, no. 11 (December 1985): 22–25; P. Bernard, "A High Flexibility Analog/Digital Library in BICMOS Technology," *Proceedings*

of *Euro ASIC* 89 (Grenoble, France: Institut National Polytechnique de Grenoble, 1989), 51–56; M. Jaslowitz, T. D'Silva, E. Zwaneveld, "Sound Genie—an Automated Digital Sound Effects Library System," *SMPTE Journal—Society of Motion Picture & Television Engineers* 99, no. 5 (May 1990): 386–91.

5. C. A. Lynch, "The Development of Electronic Publishing and Digital Library Collections on the NREN," *Electronic Networking: Research, Applications & Policy* 1, no. 2 (winter 1991): 6–22.

6. P. Graham, "Requirements for the Digital Research Library," *College & Research Libraries* 56 (July 1995): 331–39.

7. See the Digital Library Initiative, Phase 1 (1994–1998) web site (www.dli2.nsf.gov/dlione) and the Digital Library Initiative, Phase 2 (1999–2004) web site (www.dli2.nsf.gov) for detailed information on the funded projects.

8. Donald J. Waters, "What Are Digital Libraries?" *CLIR Issues,* no. 4 (July/August 1998). Available online at www.clir.org/pubs/issues/issues04.html#dlf.

9. K. M. Drabenstott, *Analytical Review of the Library of the Future* (Washington, D.C.: Council on Library Resources, 1994).

10. J. W. Dunn and C. A. Mayer, "VARIATIONS: A Digital Music Library System at Indiana University," in *DL '99: Proceedings of the Fourth ACM Conference on Digital Libraries,* Berkeley, Calif., August 1999, 12–19. See also D. Fenske and J. W. Dunn, "The VARIATIONS Project at Indiana University's Music Library," *D-Lib Magazine,* June 1996. Available online at www.dlib.org/dlib/june96/variations/06fenske.html. For more information, see the VARIATIONS web site at www.dlib.indiana.edu/variations.

11. M. Burroughs and D. Fenske, "Variations: A Hypermedia Project Providing Integrated Access to Music Information," in *Proceedings of International Computer Music Conference,* Glasgow, Scotland, 1990.

12. J. W. Dunn and C. A. Mayer, "VARIATIONS."

13. John McGinty, "Developing a Digital Library: Scale Requires Partnership," in *Choosing Our Futures: ACRL 1997 National Conference Proceedings.* Available online at www.ala.org/acrl/paperhtm/a11.html.

14. Allaire's web site can be accessed at www.allaire.com.

15. The NCSU Digital Libraries Initiatives home page is at www.lib.ncsu.edu/dli.

16. Information on Indiana University's Digital Library Program can be found at www.dlib.indiana.edu/information.

17. Eric Lease Morgan, MyLibrary: A Model for Implementing a User-Centered, Customizable Interface to a Library's Collection of Information Resources. Available online at my.lib.ncsu.edu/about/paper/index.html.

9

Perspectives of an Enlightened Vendor

PHILIP R. KESTEN

Many in the community cite Docutek Information Systems' electronic reserves software ERes as the leader among commercially available systems. This chapter lays out the history of ERes and of Docutek, and the lessons learned along the way to making the system successful and popular. As the co-creator of ERes and the co-founder of Docutek, I will tell the story in the first person.

I will also address two topics central to the evolution of electronic reserves today. One is the overlap (or lack thereof) of library systems and so-called courseware products usually offered by the instructional technology department. The other is the question so many institutions are asking—should we build our own system or buy a commercial one?

INTRODUCTION

The story of the evolution of ERes as a system and of Docutek as an entity has implications for any institution interested in using technology to automate or improve services. Whether an organization intends to purchase one or more commercial systems, hire consultants to create applications, or build systems in-house, there are pitfalls to avoid and strategies worth considering that can minimize effort and maximize results. These are discussed in the context of the development of the ERes system as well as the larger context of best practices and common experiences.

For the impatient reader, the success of ERes can be summarized in three words: agility, commitment, and partnership.

From its earliest days, Docutek as a corporate entity had an agility to respond to and incorporate emerging technologies. It wasn't encumbered by old technologies, old ways of doing things, and old solutions. As the history of the company suggests, this was partly for philosophical reasons and partly because its founders had no turf in the library community to protect. Our agility gave us the freedom to move quickly in innovative directions, resulting in a system that in many ways is greater than the sum of its parts. We were also able to move quickly in the right direction because we fostered a spirit of partnership with interested members of the library community. These partnerships helped us focus on the problems people were trying to solve and on the kinds of solutions that would be used most easily.

HISTORY OF ERes

ERes originated in the fall of 1995. The concept wasn't hatched in a corporate boardroom or described in a business plan for venture capitalists. It was born on a college campus in response to both a genuine need and the recognition that technology was more and more a driving force in academia.

In 1992, I created a software system called Phys_Chat that was used by faculty at Santa Clara and adopted at more than one hundred other institutions nationwide to facilitate course-related conversations outside the classroom.[1] Not long after its implementation, David Tauck, a faculty member in Santa Clara's Department of Biology, suggested a second use of the system, to allow instructors to make course material available electronically to students. Phys_Chat was revised to accommodate this application, and the new system was renamed "E_Res" for electronic reserves.

By mid-1995, E_Res had become popular among Santa Clara's faculty. It suffered, however, from two limitations. First, faculty and students could access the system only by logging into the campus DEC Alpha computer. In addition only text-based (ASCII) material could be distributed in E_Res, an even more restrictive constraint. Faculty who wanted to make copies of papers, articles, old exams, and homework solutions—all items commonly put on reserve in a campus library— were unable to use the system.

To me, the ideal solution to the limitations of E_Res was obvious. As a particle physicist, I had been using the World Wide Web for a number of years, and by 1995 awareness of the Web had extended well beyond physics and academia. Some excellent histories of the Internet and the Web are available in print[2,3] and on the Web.[4,5] (It's interesting to note that the concept of a server-based web was created and developed at CERN, the European Laboratory for Particle Physics.) It was clear that faculty and students would get far more benefit from E_Res by extending it to run on the Web. Nontext documents could be scanned and placed in such a system, and users could access material with nothing more than a browser and access to the Internet. Certainly the Web was the answer!

Moving E_Res to the Web was a daunting task. The system, which had a full repertoire of basic reserve features, including organization by academic course, indexing by author and subject, and a primitive archiving capability, comprised nearly 3,000 lines of FORTRAN code. And because E_Res was written to run in the relatively secure environment of a DEC Alpha—all users are required to present a valid account and password to gain access—the system had no security or authentication measures of its own. Because of the size of the conversion task, and the fact that a web-based E_Res would require some mechanism to identify authorized users, I sought out a partner to help move E_Res out of the darkness of the old ways and into the light of the Web.

I asked Slaven Zivkovic, a Santa Clara junior majoring in computer science, to join the project. He had been my student in physics, and I also worked with him when he wrote a software system we used in the campus observatory. I knew him to be exceptional with anything computer-related and probably a better software engineer than many who populate the Silicon Valley. He was enthusiastic about the idea, so we rolled up our sleeves and began to convert E_Res to run in the web environment. We changed the name of the emerging system to ERes and, a few months later, formed the company Docutek Information Systems to license it.

Ingredients for an "Enlightened" Product

The history of Docutek, outlined below, provides clues to three of the four ingredients needed to create a highly successful library system such as ERes. These three ingredients are common to any software product; only the fourth is specific to the library world.

The first ingredient in a successful system is a genuine need. Our original design and development were driven by the needs of the students, librarians, and faculty on our campus. We were lucky in that we were unencumbered by the constraints of a commercial enterprise—the need to be financially successful, for example—but the success of ERes is due largely to the fact that our primary consideration was (and is) making the system do what people really need.

The second ingredient is identifying and exploiting the appropriate technologies. Five years ago, many vendors were holding on to old, linear approaches, and, to some extent, that appears to be the case even today. But even the original version of ERes, which bears no resemblance to the current system, had a look and feel that was unmistakably new.

Textbook publishers exhibit the same tendency. As a group, they started moving five to eight years ago to incorporate multimedia and other electronic technologies into their texts and ancillary materials. Yet only recently have they begun to tap the full potential of these technologies, including the Web. Instead, they created products and systems that had the sheen of technology but offered no fundamentally new approaches to the presentation of information and no new techniques to improve the effectiveness of the material in terms of student learning. A textbook presented on a CD-ROM is still the same book. Even a CD-ROM version with key words hyperlinked to other sections of the text, while a bit easier to use, provides no functionality that cannot be similarly obtained by looking up words in the index.

Why have these two industries, library automation and textbook publishing, been relatively quick to attempt to adopt new technology but not particularly adept at employing it in efficient ways? No doubt one aspect of the answer is hesitation. Although the Internet revolution has conditioned us to expect rapid changes in every facet of our lives, the risks are high for a company that makes sudden changes away from an accepted approach.

But the primary reason companies in these areas are slow to exploit new technologies is probably a combination of unfamiliarity and momentum. Large library automation vendors and big publishing houses accumulate vast experience in developing and supporting a line of products—a good thing—but as a result, they become so focused that they can't see different approaches. In a real sense, they don't know what they don't know. In addition, the momentum of doing things a certain way for so many man-years makes it difficult to change course.

In today's technology-driven society, clocks are set to "Internet time," which one author describes as the flow of time where "people forget everything that was done six months ago."[6] Sluggishness on the part of a vendor is seen as unresponsiveness. In contrast, Docutek's agility has been key to its success as an innovator and to its being perceived by the community as enlightened. We "get it," *and* we can respond quickly enough to get new ideas into our products almost instantly.

The third ingredient, perhaps self-evident, is being able to put the right people on the job. There are many clever people who know how to write robust, high-quality software, and there are many people who understand one or another outstanding problem that requires a software solution. But relatively few people come to the table with both attributes.

Who needs to be on the team if you hope to create a successful academic- and library-related software system, and perhaps to become "enlightened" in terms of growing and supporting it? From my perspective, one needs people who are experts in software and computer technologies, who know in a deep way both the academic and library environments, and who can communicate with the librarians and faculty who work in these environments. Happily for ERes and Docutek, Zivkovic and I both have considerable experience writing large software systems, and, by virtue of my faculty position and his as a library webmaster, we were able to satisfy the other requirements.

These, then, are three of the four ingredients required to create a highly successful software system such as our ERes product: a genuine need, the ability to identify and exploit the correct technologies, and the right people. I will come to the fourth, and perhaps most critical, aspect of attaining software vendor success shortly.

HISTORY OF DOCUTEK

The original intent of my partnership with Slaven Zivkovic was to create a web-based electronic reserve system for use at Santa Clara University. But as we designed and built our ERes system, we became aware that others, both in academia and in the commercial world, were thinking about the same issues. Moreover, because it's hard to keep a secret on the Web, people outside Santa Clara became aware of our developing system. They expressed enough interest in using the results of our efforts that we would have been foolish not to consider a financial enterprise. Docutek Information Systems was formed as a partnership company in the fall of 1995.

The first version of ERes, which we later referred to as ERes v1.0, was completed in late 1995. By the next summer, ERes v2.0—the first commercial version—was being installed in the United States and in Australia. Our marketing was limited to word of mouth and to seeking out apparent comrades in arms through web searches.

Early on, we came across a sociology professor, Manfred Kuechler at Hunter College (City College of New York), who had a similar interest in putting course documents online. At the time, he was writing a paper on the issues involved in creating and using an "innovative instructional tool" that he called an electronic reserve shelf.[7] We began a fruitful dialogue on electronic reserves and offered a discounted copy of ERes to Hunter College in exchange for his comments and suggestions. With his acceptance, the first of several partnerships between Docutek and the academic community was formed.

Less than a week after our initial conversation with Manfred Kuechler, a librarian from Bucknell University, Bud Hiller, wrote an unsolicited request for information on ERes. Bucknell, he said, was in the process of "looking seriously at putting together electronic reserves." As the administrator of the reserve desk, Hiller was in the ideal position not only to tell us what he needed—to be able to put articles scanned to PDF format onto the Web, for example—but also to compare our system with options from other vendors. Within only a few months, ERes was up and running at Bucknell, but even before that, we felt a spirit of partnership with Hiller and his Bucknell colleagues.

We did not consider Hunter College and Bucknell University as beta sites. We had done as thorough a job on quality assurance testing as possible before release, and ERes had been in beta mode at Santa Clara for an extended period before we began to license it to schools like Hunter and Bucknell. It's true that they identified a number of problems (bugs) for us to fix (there were a few problems with the system when we initially released it), but our ERes v1.0 was not a demo version sent out to be field-tested. Nonetheless, the feedback that Hiller and Professor Kuechler provided regarding the functionality of the system was invaluable. They told us how to make what was already in the system work better for librarians and faculty and suggested the kinds of features that people on the front lines really needed.

As the popularity of ERes grew, other loose partnerships formed between Docutek and librarians using the system. Bob Fraser at the University of Michigan-Dearborn, for example, has offered us the benefit of his experience many times since Dearborn adopted ERes in the fall of 1997. Relationships like the ones we have with Manfred Kuechler, Bud Hiller, Bob Fraser, and others are at the heart of the fourth and most important ingredient required for creating a successful product and for being viewed as an "enlightened" vendor. That ingredient is an abiding interest in what the community needs and a willingness to act when the community speaks. Many commercial enterprises work with customers in order to make products more marketable—most vendors gather beta sites and user groups—but from our perspective, the *only* goal was a better system.

I don't know if it's true with other vendors, but at Docutek we work just as much with schools and libraries that are not customers as with those that are. In at least a few cases, there was never even a possibility that the school with which we were working on a particular issue would ever become a Docutek customer. The rapid development of our access statistics package came about in this way, and recently we completely revised the copyright document management system based largely on comments from schools not currently using the system.

Through word of mouth and by virtue of a small press table presence at the American Library Association annual meeting in San Francisco in the summer of 1997, awareness of our system grew. The number of ERes systems increased steadily. Docutek also grew, and by the end of 1998 a number of part-time technical staff and consultants had been brought on board to contribute to technical support and new product development. However, no one at Docutek was prepared for the explosion of interest in ERes in early 1999. The number of schools using ERes nearly doubled in less than nine months.

In response to the explosion of interest in ERes, Docutek hired two full-time software engineers, incorporated, and began to seek funding for expansion. By the end of the summer of 1999, an initial management team was in place, with Walter Sousa, formerly the chairman and chief executive officer of AT&T Asia Pacific, serving as chairman of the board of directors. Nathan Vince, formerly the vice president, worldwide sales of Astec, Plc., joined Docutek as chief executive officer, and funding from high-profile technology investors in both Silicon Valley and Asia closed in January 2000.

The changes in Docutek notwithstanding, we have been aggressive in ensuring that the four ingredients described above remain active elements in the way we conduct business. In particular, we have placed a high priority on maintaining the strength we draw from input from the library community. In addition to the many informal partnerships we have developed over the years, Docutek recently formed a board of advisors drawn from libraries and library organizations across the country. The membership of the board is a veritable who's who of the library world: Charles Beard, director of libraries at the State University of West Georgia; Alice Calabrese, executive director of the Chicago Library System; Fred Heath, dean of the university libraries at Texas A&M University; James G. Neal, dean of libraries at Johns Hopkins University; Maureen Pastine, librarian at Temple University; Roy Tennant, manager for e-scholarship web and services design in the California Digital Library; and James F. Williams II, dean of libraries at the University of Colorado at Boulder. We look to this group to guide the development of new features and new products that enable libraries to harness the academic power of technology. This capacity is the future of academic libraries and, therefore, the future of Docutek.

ON THE OVERLAP OF THE LIBRARY AND INSTRUCTIONAL TECHNOLOGY

It is becoming increasingly common on college and university campuses for the library, the computing unit, the media services group, and the instructional technology department to attempt to work together. On some campuses, some or all of these groups have been merged. Although librarians and instructional technologists at many schools believe this kind of interaction will benefit students, it's not always a smooth road.

Perhaps the most significant source of contention between the library and instructional technology is in the overlap, or perceived overlap, of electronic reserves and web-based courses. Companies like WebCT and Blackboard.com offer so-called courseware products that facilitate the creation of web sites for academic courses, and one component of these, naturally, is the ability to put readings and other course documents online. At first glance, this would also seem to be the main purpose of an electronic reserves system. Is there a conflict here?

I don't believe that a true conflict exists between courseware and electronic reserves. Many sites use both a courseware product and ERes, and reports indicate that both are being used effectively. Many schools are also using ERes as both a courseware product and an electronic reserve system, but this is not a requirement of our system.

Courseware products are aimed directly at faculty. They do not provide features that deal with copyright or that write MARC records to allow course material to be cataloged properly. In addition, whereas courseware products present every course as a self-contained unit, many libraries are approaching course material from the perspective of whole disciplines, for example, by researching resources available on the network and organizing them by subject. Although some overlap in functionality exists between a system like ERes and a courseware product, the library cannot meet all needs with a courseware system. There is no conflict: A system like DocuLib/ERes is required to allow libraries to web-enable the services they have traditionally offered.

BUILD VERSUS BUY

To satisfy the increasingly clear need to put reserve material on the Web, many academic libraries are choosing to build a homegrown system rather than purchase a commercial one. As a vendor of a commercial system I have a vested interest in the outcomes of decisions like this. However, since ERes can rightly be classified as homegrown, at least at its roots, my perspective is not necessarily vendor-centric.

Building a system rather than buying one is an attractive option for two reasons. First, homegrown systems can be developed at an actual or apparently lower cost. Second, building a system enables a library to retain complete local control of the system design and implementation. On the other hand, commercial systems can offer a larger feature set, feature enhancements, and other improvements. Vendors provide stronger system support than can usually be provided locally, and commercial systems are less likely to break.

The answers to these critical questions clarify the issues germane to the build-versus-buy decision:

What is involved in getting an electronic reserve project off the ground?

How long does it take from project start until the system can be placed into active service?

What is the real cost to the library, including ongoing maintenance?

What features will likely be available in the system?

How will the system be supported?

What is the long-term outlook for the system—will it be reliable, and will new features be easily added as its use evolves?

In order to make an apples to apples comparison, it is necessary to distinguish between a homegrown electronic reserve *system* and a much less functional approach that some schools are taking. In libraries where the goal is simply to have online links to web-based documents, a straightforward and effective technique is to add a URL to the 856 field in an item's MARC record stored in the online catalog. Indeed, the 856 field is called the "electronic location and access" field, and it was apparently introduced for the specific purpose of allowing a MARC record to link to a web-served document.[8] However, using the 856 field in this way offers none of the other features that many libraries seek in a reserve system, such as copyright management, document tracking, and document security. For this reason, I will not consider the 856-field approach in the discussion that follows.

What is involved in getting an electronic reserve project off the ground?

The initial process necessary to implement a basic homegrown system can be as straightforward as having a few planning meetings and then designating the staff or hiring the students to do the development. This initial phase of the project can therefore be relatively quick and uncomplicated at most institutions, made considerably easier by the wealth of community experience with electronic reserves accumulated over the last few years. Even just three or four years ago, considerable effort might have been invested in determining the appropriate feature set and logical organization of an electronic reserves system. Today, hundreds of examples exist on which to base a new project.

When the goal is to select a commercial system, however, my experience at both Docutek and Santa Clara University suggests that the initial process takes a moderate to long amount of time. A number of vendors are often scheduled for on-campus presentations. Due diligence requires committee meetings and the checking of reliable references. The decision-making process is likely to be lengthy and involved.

In light of these considerations, with respect to the time and complexity of getting an electronic reserves project launched, I give the edge to homegrown systems.

How long does it take from project start until the system can be placed into active service?

Implementation time—the time it takes to design, create, and test a system—depends on the number and depth of the intended features and the expected functionality of the system. A basic system with minimal functionality can be implemented in as little as one month. As an example, the authors of the FreeReserves system developed at Southern Illinois University, Carbondale, which offers only a create, an input, and a limited index capability, report that initial coding was done in fifty man-hours.[9]

Writing the software, of course, is only one component of the total system implementation. My experience with large software applications is that the time to design the system and the time to create the software are about the same, and that the time to test and debug is about equal to the time to design and write the software put together. The time required to design FreeReserves and then to test it after coding was complete is not reported, but, given this observation, the total implementation time for this system was probably about two hundred hours. Even if that is an overestimate, one hundred to two hundred hours for implementation is a reasonable lower limit.

Not all attempts to build an in-house system end with a finished product. A number of schools have either privately or publicly reported unsatisfactory experiences in trying to build their own systems. For various reasons, schools like UC San Diego and UC Santa Cruz each terminated attempts to develop in-house web systems, at the expense of as many as two man-years of nonproductive effort. Both of these institutions are large enough to have access to in-house technical expertise, but in UCSD's case that actually contributed to the project's demise. Kathy Whitley, formerly of the Science and Engineering Library at UCSD, told me they had a "crack programmer" on the project, but this person couldn't make fast progress due to other responsibilities. He was eventually hired away by industry and replaced by advanced student programmers. "But," Whitley says, "they graduated and went on to lucrative industry jobs. We had the commitment from the library management, but our biggest problem was retaining high-level programming staff. I gather this is a problem throughout academia."

Certainly, the more complex the system—that is, the more features required and the higher the quality demanded of the user interface—the longer the implementation time. Experience dictates that each of the three phases—design, building, and testing—is proportional to the complexity of the system. As an example, over eight thousand man-hours are already invested in the design, building, and testing of Docutek's DocuLib/ERes system.

For a commercial system, implementation time should be short. For example, it typically takes a few days for a library to collect the information we require to customize a DocuLib/ERes system. After that, the customization, pre-installation testing, and installation require about two weeks.

In light of these considerations, I give the edge to a commercial product with respect to the time required to implement an electronic reserve system once a decision has been made to move forward.

What is the real cost to the library, including ongoing maintenance?

By far the single most significant factor in the cost to develop a homegrown system is the salary of staff, students, or consultants who design and create the software. This is often a hidden or "sunk" cost, however, and in most cases no budget process is required. As a result, the price tag to develop a homegrown system may appear to be much lower than the real cost to the library. A recent survey of a selected group of ARL libraries drives this point home. In her summary of the survey, Cindy Kristof of Kent State University writes, "The sixteen libraries that developed their own 'homegrown' web-based system spent an average of $7,989 on hardware and $969 on software."[10] I am no longer amazed by the second figure, but when I mention it to business folks—

members of Docutek's board of directors, for example—the response is usually incredulity. Even at $15 per hour, a very low estimate of the wage one might pay students averaged with the salary of a member of the library staff serving as a supervisor, $969 covers about sixty-five hours of work. It's hard to believe that the real cost to develop a home-grown electronic reserve system could be this low; the conclusion is that the most significant factor—wages—was hidden and therefore not included by the survey respondents.

Using student labor does not significantly reduce the cost to develop a large software application. Experience suggests that development costs are the same regardless of whether staff or students do the work: While student time is cheaper than staff or consultant time, students can't do the design work and must be supervised during the creation and testing phases.

As with system development, wages are the primary contributor to the cost of ongoing maintenance. Moreover, it is a generally held tenet among academic computing units that of all the aspects of building any computer-based system in-house, by far the largest cost is for maintenance.[11] The two primary reasons are that there is rarely institutionalized support for ongoing maintenance, so support is done haphazardly and is reactive rather than preventive, and that detailed knowledge of the system can quickly be lost when any original principal is no longer associated with the project. The second reason is of particular importance when students or consultants are employed to build the system.

Based on the numbers outlined here, a basic reserve system like FreeReserves, with an estimated time of two hundred hours to design, build, and test, would cost between $3,000 and $6,000 in staff wages. Ongoing annual maintenance would at least be on the same order, so this figure of $3,000 to $6,000 would be an annual amount. This does not include the cost of administering the system.

It is harder to quantify the cost of a commercial system because some are stand-alone while others are embedded within a larger system such as an online public access catalog (OPAC). Costs vary considerably from one vendor to another, and there is no one-size-fits-all system on the market.

I can compare costs with those associated with Docutek's Docu-Lib/ERes system. With no consortium-based discount, a new installation of DocuLib/ERes carries a minimum annual license of $2,500 plus an additional amount based on student enrollment and optional add-on modules selected. A school of average size that selects one optional add-on module would pay an annual site license fee of approximately $4,100. In addition, there is a one-time $5,000 setup, customization, and installation fee. Costs for DocuLib/ERes therefore average $9,100 in year one and $4,100 in subsequent years. This does not include the cost of administering the system.

In light of these considerations, there is no clear-cut winner between homegrown and commercial in terms of the cost of an electronic reserve system. For certain schools and certain system specifics, either alternative might prove to be the least expensive.

What features will likely be available in the system?

Certainly, one potential advantage of building a system locally is the ability to customize it to the exact requirements of the institution. In some cases, this may be a primary factor in deciding to create a homegrown system—issues important to the local community and special needs dictated by the local environment or culture can be specifically addressed.

On the other hand, too narrow a focus can lead to a myopic perspective that limits an in-house system. Even with the higher visibility of electronic reserves and other applications of technology in today's library, a system builder who looks only inward may fail to notice effective, innovative ideas developed at other institutions. Many ERes features that were added at the suggestion of one school or another have generated a "why didn't I think of that?!" response from other ERes institutions. A few that come quickly to mind are the ability to share documents between courses, an interface to manage the collection of Internet resources, and a "virtual reference librarian."

A homegrown system will by definition include the ability to post documents to the Web. Some method for organizing the documents, either through the catalog or by means of an indexing scheme embedded in the application, must also be available. Features beyond these are optional, and whether or not any are included depends on the interest and expertise of the system designers and builders, as well as the amount of time dedicated to the project. In my experience, homegrown systems tend toward the more basic.

Another drawback of a homegrown system in terms of the feature set stems from the fact that, except for the largest institutions, it is difficult for schools to develop partnerships with OPAC, full-text database, and other vendors. In the evolution from a basic documents database to a more robust electronic reserve system, to the web-enabling of other related library services, partnerships with vendors of OPAC systems, full-text online databases, and other library technologies play an increasingly significant role.

There are other drawbacks. First, the more complex the feature set, the more involved and costly the implementation. In addition, the technical expertise required to develop features such as a fully functional copyright-protected database tracking and management system may be beyond the scope of the average technical library staff or students.

Unlike a homegrown system, which can be tailored to meet local requirements, the feature set in a commercial product will not be specific to an institution. In the case of Docutek's DocuLib/ERes, some customization is available and new features are added frequently in response to requests from users. DocuLib is also modular, allowing an institution to select the subset of features appropriate to its needs. This may or may not satisfy some specific need presented by a given institution.

In general, though, one should expect a wide array of features in a commercial reserves system. For example, DocuLib/ERes includes features that allow complete copyright tracking and management—including automatic letter creation for contacting rights holders—real-time, online reference services, electronic document delivery, and document input via fax. Technical expertise and considerable effort are required to incorporate complex features like these into a system, so it is unlikely that any but a commercial product will offer them.

Even simpler features and basic system niceties are unlikely to be found in a homegrown system. Having watched the development of scores of projects in academia for over two decades, I have observed that the nonessentials are always left for a future round of improvements that, in many cases, never happens. Features like date-stamping and usage reports, which are standard fare in ERes, may never find their way into a homegrown system.

In my opinion, it is in the feature set that the commercial system wins out over a homegrown one. Even if a basic system initially satisfies a library's needs, any limitations will only become more obvious and more confining as time goes on. A good commercial reserve system, on the other hand, should provide the library with the advanced as well as the basic, enabling efficient use of the system right from the start as well as the opportunity to grow as use of the technology evolves.

How will the system be supported?

Support for the software component of any homegrown electronic reserve system must necessarily be provided in-house. Effective support requires familiarity with the details of both the software and the database around which the system is built. It is therefore unlikely that any but those people who developed the system will be able to keep it running efficiently. It's not impossible, of course, to train someone new to be able to support the system later on. But one of the biggest advantages of having applications written by professional software engineers is that, on the whole, the code is organized, easy to read, and easier to maintain. Homegrown code often does not evidence the same level of organization, so it may be difficult to bring new people in to support an in-house system. This becomes even more of a complication as the principals of the system development leave for other projects or, in the case of students, graduate.

Hardware support is often also provided in-house, although more and more institutions are choosing to outsource campus-wide hardware support to an external organization. In-house support may come from one or more people on the library staff dedicated to or partially responsible for things technological. At some institutions, hardware support is covered by the information technology/computing unit on campus, the quality of which may depend on the relationship between the library and the computing people. In any event, each possibility carries potential advantages and disadvantages; only in a specific situation can this aspect of homegrown versus commercial systems be completely analyzed.

One expected advantage of a commercial system, on the other hand, is that the software should be completely supported by the vendor. Docutek, for example, includes total software support as part of the standard annual license. Depending on the hardware required for a particular reserve system, the vendor may or may not provide support for the hardware as well as the software. At Docutek, because our DocuLib/ERes systems run on small web server computers, for example, Pentium-based PC computers, we do not provide direct hardware support. However, our technical team provides consulting on hardware issues at no extra charge.

In light of these considerations, with respect to system support I give the edge to a commercial product.

What is the long-term outlook for the system— will it be reliable, and will new features be easily added as its use evolves?

Obviously, the more complex the application, the more likely that bugs and other generic system weaknesses will be present. And even the most basic electronic reserve system requires more than a few programs; FreeReserves, for example, includes twelve separate Perl language scripts and three directories.[12] However, because quality assurance is time-consuming and tedious, it almost always receives the least attention during implementation. Moreover, a technical background alone is not a sufficient qualification to carry out successful quality assurance. The most insidious software bugs have a way of remaining hidden unless a specific set of circumstances occurs, so finding them demands experience in quality assurance testing as well as technical expertise. This is perhaps the most serious potential pitfall of homegrown systems because it can result in an unexpected crisis. In the worst-case scenario, hidden defects in the software can result in a catastrophic loss of database information required to access documents in the system, or of the documents themselves.

One should rightly expect, on the other hand, that a commercial system has been thoroughly tested before release. DocuLib/ERes, for example, has been subjected to extensive quality assurance testing. That's not to say that no bugs will be found after a vendor installs a new system, but these system defects ought to be minor or infrequent.

Field experience and direct reports from a large user base have provided conclusive evidence that DocuLib/ERes is robust and not subject to database corruption or software-based data loss.

The arguments regarding system support can be applied to the issue of system evolution. Because the details of system architecture are often lost a year or two after the initial implementation, as the staff or students who built the system move on, it is sometimes difficult or impractical to augment an in-house system with new features and functionality.

A solid commercial system, on the other hand, should be completely scalable, and enhancements should be expected as technology changes. Over the five years since the first commercial version of ERes, for example, we have frequently offered feature enhancements, and full system upgrades have been released on a timetable that is reasonable for the rate at which technology has changed.

In light of these considerations, commercial products have a clear advantage with respect to the long-term reliability and evolution of an electronic reserve system.

BUILD VERSUS BUY: CONCLUSIONS

The build-versus-buy discussion can be summarized in terms of the advantages and disadvantages of each.

The advantages of a homegrown electronic reserves system include:

- Basic system can be created quickly.
- Decision-making process is simpler; little or no high-level administrative action is required.
- Cost is lower, or apparently lower.
- Design is controlled locally.

The disadvantages of a homegrown system include:

- Actual cost is obscured; most costs are wages and are therefore hidden.
- Fully featured systems require a long development time.
- Time and expertise limitations often force systems to be limited in features and integrity.
- Technical support is limited.
- Long-term technical support is limited.
- It is difficult to incorporate new technologies.

The advantages of a commercial electronic reserve system include:

- Implementation time after decision is short.
- Value-to-cost ratio is high.
- Systems offer full feature sets.
- Enhancements keep pace with changes in technology.

- Vendors offer high level of support.
- Long-term support is available.

The disadvantages of a commercial system include:

- Time for vendor and system selection can be long.
- Cost is higher, or perceived as higher.
- Feature set may not exactly match local requirements.

Based on this analysis, I feel that the best choice for most libraries is a commercial system. Real cost in either case is comparable, and the commercial system should be more robust, should provide a larger and more powerful feature set, and should be better supported.

CLOSING REMARKS

When we started to create ERes more than five years ago, some academic libraries had electronic reserve systems running, and a few were piloting web-based systems. The technology leaders in libraries had been discussing the subject at ALA meetings on the e-reserve discussion list, but interest in web reserves was only just becoming widespread. The field has changed enormously since then, and it has been both exhilarating and immensely rewarding to witness the explosion in the deployment of electronic reserves systems and to have played a small role in it.

NOTES

1. P. R. Kesten, "An Electronic Study Group," *Council on Undergraduate Research Quarterly* 15 (1994): 105–7.
2. John December, *The World Wide Web 1997 Unleashed,* 4th ed. (Indianapolis: Sams, 1997).
3. Art Wolinsky, *The History of the Internet and the World Wide Web* (Berkeley Heights, N.J.: Enslow, 1999).
4. Robert Cailliau, A Short History of the Web, www.inria.fr/Actualites/ Cailliau-fra.html, 1995.
5. Barry M. Leiner, et al., A Brief History of the Internet, www.isoc.org/ internet-history/brief.html, 2000.

6. George Parker, "Creative Impulse" (column), *Marketing Computers,* April 2000.

7. Manfred Kuechler, "The Electronic Reserve Shelf (ERS)—Using the WWW as a Teaching Resource," talk given at American Sociological Association meeting (Sociology and Computers section), New York, July 1996.

8. Eric Lease Morgan, "The World Wide Web and Mosaic: An Overview for Librarians," *The Public-Access Computer Systems Review* 5, no. 6 (1994): 5–26.

9. Shane A. Nackerud, "E-Reserves: Home Grown vs. Turnkey," talk given at ACRL Annual Conference, Detroit, April 1999.

10. Cindy Kristof, "Electronic Reserves Operations in ARL Libraries," 027.7 Sp74, no. 245 (SPEC Flyer) (Washington, D.C.: Association of Research Libraries, Office of Leadership and Management Services, 1999).

11. Private communication, Carl Fussell, co-director, Information Technology, Santa Clara University, Santa Clara, Calif.

12. Shane A. Nackerud, "E-Reserve."

10

Perspective of the Association of Research Libraries

MARY E. JACKSON

The Association of Research Libraries (ARL) has monitored the emergence, acceptance, and introduction of electronic reserve services in research and academic libraries since the early 1990s. ARL's mission is to shape and influence forces affecting the future of research libraries in the process of scholarly communication. ARL's interest in electronic reserve services falls clearly within one of the association's eight strategic objectives: to make access to research resources more efficient and effective. In the 1990s, research and academic libraries were faced with a number of now well-documented pressures (explosion in published material, skyrocketing cost of that material, increase in the number of users, and changes in the nature of instructional support). ARL's response to those pressures was to develop new ways of strengthening performance of research libraries, develop methods to introduce and use emergent forms of electronic information, and form strategic alliances with other higher education agencies.

Traditionally, research libraries have provided a specialized location within the library for faculty-chosen course readings. Many research libraries have established separate reserve libraries within their main library buildings. These reserve libraries have been print-based but include a variety of types of materials. Access to what is in the reserve library has been via print or online course lists. Some libraries provide open access to books and hold the photocopies behind a service desk; others house all reserve materials behind service desks. Materials are generally checked out for short periods of time, as short as two hours in some cases, and fines are high for materials not returned by the due date. The collection changes each semester in response to new courses.

The weaknesses of the print-based reserve library or reserve book room are obvious: faculty submission of readings sometimes weeks after the semester has begun; labor-intensive library processing routines to put materials on reserve; limited hours of access for the students; very intense demand for material for short periods of time; cyclical use; and a higher-than-average loss or damage rate that suggests students do not want to be restricted by short loan periods and high fines.

The emergence of an electronic alternative to the print-based reserve system offered the potential to eliminate or minimize many of these weaknesses. An electronic reserve system was defined as "liberation from the tyranny of space and time" in that it provided storage of material in electronic format; provided electronic access, retrieval, viewing, downloading, and printing; and provided access beyond the library's walls and during times the library was closed. This description is likely very similar to that in other chapters in this collection. Research and academic libraries were looking for methods to improve instructional support of materials of the highest quality to students at the lowest possible cost. They were seeking ways to improve access for students while gaining efficiencies in their processing.

EARLY COLLABORATION WITH THE NATIONAL ASSOCIATION OF COLLEGE STORES

In 1994 and 1995, the Association of Research Libraries and the National Association of College Stores (NACS) co-sponsored three forums devoted to the topic of electronic reserves. The title of the forums, "Electronic Reserves: Developing New Partnerships to Provide Support in an Electronic Age," highlighted the potential for libraries to collaborate with other agencies within the university. The aim of the forums was to explore how the evolving nature of the instructional support services in academic institutions could be supported by electronic reserve capabilities. In the mid-1990s, many libraries were just beginning to explore the area of electronic reserves, and the events gave attendees a unique opportunity to explore and discuss this emerging alternative to their print-based service.

Each forum featured presentations by the pioneering libraries that were offering electronic reserve services: San Diego State University, Colorado State University (CSU), Duke University, Rice University, Northwestern University, and Rensselaer Polytechnic Institute. At the time, these systems were state of the art, but a quick skim of their descriptions confirms how far the hardware and software have evolved. Colorado State's "RESERVE ONLINE!" included approximately twenty-five to thirty items in the text-based system. Colorado State's Tom Delaney developed the software that ran on an IBM RISC 16000. Duke used Xerox's Document on Demand system, which stored approximately two thousand nine hundred items. Rice also developed its own system that supported six courses with approximately twenty to thirty items per course. San Diego State, the first to offer an electronic reserve system in January 1992, used E-RBR, by Nousoft, Inc., and reported over three thousand items for over four hundred courses.

PRESENTATIONS AT THREE ELECTRONIC RESERVE FORUMS

Many of the presentations by early implementers included summaries of their copyright policies. All libraries included material provided by faculty, such as course notes, problem sets, exams, and other non-copyrighted items. Some libraries also included copies of journal articles and book chapters and considered use of such copyrighted material to be fair use. Each event included a presentation on copyright by Laura Gasaway as well as small group discussions that explored the copyright "comfort zone."

The electronic reserve forums also included presentations by publishers and bookstore representatives. An article in the fall 1994 issue of *PSP Bulletin* summarized portions of the presentation given by Lois Wasoff (Houghton Mifflin Company) at the July 1994 forum. She noted that "electronic reserve rooms differ from traditional reserve rooms in ways which present both legal issues and business challenges." She characterized systems that acknowledge the rights of publishers and authors to be compensated for their efforts as "extremely positive," but she warned that "if electronic reserve rooms are not configured with an awareness of the rights of copyright owners and the legal and financial responsibilities of users, they can become a serious threat to the continued viability of the publishing industry and its contribution to creativity and scholarship."[1] Wasoff articulated a view held by many commercial publishers; that is, digital copying is quite different from photocopying. She asserted that "the bulk of the uses made of the copyright works in an electronic reserve context—involving as they do the *reproduction* and *distribution of significant portions* of copyright works in a manner which is likely to have *a negative effect on the actual or potential market* for the copyrighted work—are not fair use and require permission from the copyright owner."[2] (emphasis in the original text)

Dan Archer represented the University of Southern California Bookstore at the March 1995 forum. The title of his presentation, "Partnerships in Service That Make Cents," underscored the importance of the economic argument and the increasingly divergent views of electronic reserves held by libraries and bookstores. Some attendees interpreted Archer's title to mean that electronic reserves should generate income rather than being reasonably priced. He cited several benefits of collaboration to the USC library, including copyright clearance, file maintenance and payments, reduction in the number of individual items that needed to be tracked by the library, and an increase in the number of classes served without a concomitant increase in reserve library workload. He also noted benefits to the bookstore, including additional course readers and approximately $155,000 in annual additional sales. The increased volume permitted bookstores to negotiate additional discounts from the print vendors. Some bookstore representatives believed that the coursepacks offered by bookstores were identical in content to what was being offered in the emerging electronic reserve services, while some librarians were of the opinion that there was minimal overlap in content. Without data on the overlap, it was difficult for librarians to accept the recommendation (intentional in Archer's presentation or not) to seek copyright permission for all materials put into an electronic reserve system.

COPYRIGHT EMERGES AS THE KEY ISSUE

These first three electronic reserve conferences brought to light the emerging, and increasingly divergent, views of the single issue that was to shape discussions between librarians and copyright holders over the remainder of the 1990s: differing interpretations of copyright for electronic reserves.

Laura Gasaway's copyright presentations at the three conferences summarized the views held by librarians with respect to electronic reserves:

> Libraries generally followed the American Library Association's (ALA) *Model Policy Concerning College and University Photocopying for Classroom, Research, and Library Reserve Use* for print-based reserve collections.
>
> Copyright for reserves falls under section 107, not section 108, of the Copyright Act.
>
> The Copyright Act is technology neutral; thus supplying an electronic copy to a user presents the same copyright issues as those involved in supplying a photocopy.

Gasaway's early presentations noted the lack of consensus on whether electronic reserves are fair use, but she argued that if libraries seek permission from publishers and pay royalties if asked, they would be giving up fair-use rights. The question of whether electronic reserve services are covered by fair use was at the heart of the discussions at the Conference on Fair Use, or CONFU.

SEEKING TO DEVELOP CONSENSUS GUIDELINES: THE CONFERENCE ON FAIR USE

In July 1994, the working group on intellectual property rights of the Information Infrastructure Task Force (IITF) released a draft of *Intellectual Property and the National Information Infrastructure* (the green paper), which called for only minor changes to the Copyright Act of 1976. In September 1994, the working group convened a conference on fair-use issues and launched a three-year process to develop guidelines for fair uses of copyrighted works by and in libraries and educational settings. If consensus could be reached, the working group expected to endorse the guidelines and include them in its final report.[3] More than eighty organizations representing libraries, publishers, multimedia centers, and educational communities participated in the general CONFU process at one point or another.

Issue papers and fair-use scenarios were written for some twenty topics, including electronic reserves. After reviewing the papers, participants agreed to organize working groups to draft guidelines for electronic reserves, interlibrary loan, distance education, visual images, and multimedia. Many of the smaller, issue-based working groups ranged from ten to twenty active participants.

The working group on electronic reserves was chaired by Kenneth Crews of Indiana University-Purdue University Indianapolis (IUPUI) and included representatives from libraries, library associations, publishers, and educational institutions. Their lively discussions in meetings during 1995 resulted in several drafts but no formal agreement on the content of the guidelines.

ARL distributed various drafts to its member leaders for review and comment. As early as mid-1995, ARL members expressed concern that the draft electronic reserve guidelines would:

   restrict access to students registered in the class (e.g., narrow current access that serves all students in the institution);

   place very restrictive technological limits on access to materials (e.g., limit access from dedicated workstations in the library);

   impose strict limitations on the proportion of course materials included (e.g., not all course materials assigned for reserve could be included);

   impose strict limitations on the type of material (e.g., limit materials to only supplemental readings and prohibit inclusion of required readings); and

   limit electronic access to one term (e.g., require permission for reuse).[4]

These concerns and those raised by other CONFU participants, including serious reservations by publisher representatives, were sent to the electronic reserves working group for consideration. Compromises were developed and discussed, but the group reached an impasse at the end of 1995. It concluded that consensus on a set of guidelines would not be possible. Representatives of copyright holders and users could not agree on what should be included in, or excluded from, electronic reserve guidelines. In fact, some individuals could not even agree on the concept of electronic reserves. Some copyright holders believe that electronic reserve services are simply electronic coursepacks for which royalties are paid on all component articles. In January 1996, a smaller group representing scholarly societies, university presses, and library associations tried to revitalize the process; the group issued draft guidelines in March 1996 and solicited comments from members of the participating associations as well as all CONFU participants.

At the May 1996 CONFU meeting, it was clear that participants were unable to ensure that fair-use guidelines would emerge for any of the four topics (interlibrary loan, electronic reserves, distance education, and multimedia). Representatives of the library and education communities believed the drafts were too strict; some commercial publishers believed they were too lenient. Some participants even questioned whether voluntarily negotiated guidelines do guarantee a "safe harbor" for educational institutions. These discussions underscored the divergent assumptions about whether these new guidelines would provide any assurance against legal action. It also became clear that there was a philosophical disagreement among CONFU participants about whether the guidelines should define maximum or minimum standards. Several librarians overseeing electronic reserve operations in ARL member libraries also echoed their concern on the arl-ereserve discussion list by wondering if the guidelines were all that libraries could do or the minimum that would allow libraries to push the envelope. Does the current copyright law permit an appropriate interpretation for electronic reserve operations?

A majority of participants at the November 1996 CONFU plenary meeting rejected the March 1996 draft of electronic reserve guidelines because there was no general consensus that the document represented an understanding of fair use by all participants.

Based on review of the various drafts by ARL member libraries and recommendations from the ARL copyright issues working group, the ARL board of directors decided not to endorse the various CONFU proposals. In May 1996, the board rejected the proposal for educational multimedia and in July of that year decided not to endorse what became the final draft of the electronic reserve guidelines. (The Association of American Publishers and the Software Publishers Association also rejected the guidelines in 1996.) In May 1997, the board rejected the final proposals for distance learning and digital images. Responding to the restrictive limitations that recurred in the various drafts and final proposals, the ARL board affirmed that ARL should not endorse any copyright guidelines that do not fully protect the fair-use rights of the scholarly and educational communities.

Three themes emerged from the ARL member library comment on all of the draft CONFU guidelines:

1. The quantitative limitations and restrictions included in the proposals unduly narrow the interpretation of fair use by moving away from the four factor analysis that is specified in section 107 of the Copyright Act of 1976.
2. Guidelines as rigid and specific as those being proposed are premature given the rapid evolution of new technologies and the lack of experience in the areas in which proposals were being considered.
3. The proposals are technically and administratively burdensome to libraries and their institutions because they add new responsibilities and raise new liability issues.[5]

The IITF white paper acknowledged that although policy considerations could suggest a regulatory or legislative solution, the working group chose to wait for the final reports of CONFU before articulating its position. The final report suggested that fair use might be more narrowly interpreted in the future. It noted that fair use was a "murky" limitation and suggested metering as a way of tracking use. It referenced the *Texaco* case in which copies were available at "reasonable cost" through the Copyright Clearance Center.

The U.S. Patent and Trademark Office, sponsor of the Conference on Fair Use, issued two reports. The first, in September 1997, was at the conclusion of the first phase of the Conference on Fair Use.[6] The second, in November 1998, was the final report.[7]

Some librarians have worried that without the CONFU guidelines, the concept of fair use will be lost in the electronic reserve environment. One librarian even suggested that it would be easier to acquiesce to a system that requires libraries to seek permission for every use of every article or chapter, pay royalties on most of them, and revert to paper backup copies for those for which libraries cannot obtain permission or the royalties are exorbitant. If this happened, would research and academic libraries be limited to providing print-based reserve services?

Guidelines for electronic reserves were published in the working group's final report, but they remain unendorsed and unlegislated. Because the drafts were widely disseminated, some academic libraries have informally implemented the CONFU guidelines in the belief that they provide a reasonable framework for their electronic reserve operations. If a sufficient number of libraries follow the unendorsed guidelines, they might become the "unofficial law."

The Association of Research Libraries participated in the Conference on Fair Use believing that the process would capture for the digital environment the carefully constructed balance that has been achieved and maintained in the print environment. ARL's rejection of the various CONFU draft guidelines confirms that they did not achieve that delicate balance of maintaining the rights of users and those of authors, publishers, and copyright owners.

FAIR USE IN THE ELECTRONIC AGE: SERVING THE PUBLIC INTEREST

In January 1995, in the midst of the CONFU discussions, ARL and representatives from five other library associations issued a draft statement titled *Fair Use in the Electronic Age: Serving the Public Interest.*[8] The ARL board of directors endorsed the statement in February 1995 and encouraged its distribution to spark discussions about fair use in the electronic age. The statement outlined lawful uses of copyrighted works in both the print and electronic environments. It noted, "Without infringing copyright, nonprofit libraries and other section 108 libraries, on behalf of their clientele, should be able . . . to provide copyrighted materials as part of electronic reserve room services."

The inclusion of electronic reserves in this statement was yet another articulation of ARL's belief that the Copyright Act of 1976 protects electronic reserve services. The statement reaffirmed the library associations' strong belief in the balance between the rights of users and those of authors, publishers, and copyright owners.

POST-CONFU: ARE GUIDELINES NEEDED?

Do libraries need guidelines? David Green, executive director of the National Initiative for a Networked Cultural Heritage, outlined his views on the CONFU process after the final meeting in May 1997.[9] He asked, "What are the bedrock principles that could serve the nonprofit community in the place of broadly accepted guidelines?" He suggested that, "having attempted to play fair through CONFU, it is time to reassert fair use at the legislative level."

The June 1997 issue of *ARL,* a special issue on copyright, also reported on a post-CONFU initiative. The Association of Research Libraries, American Library Association, American Association of Law Libraries, Special Libraries Association, and Medical Library Association agreed on a series of efforts to encourage the development, use, and sharing of fair-use policies and practices within the educational setting. One of the suggestions was to assist in developing user community principles and educator- and librarian-generated best practices concerning fair use. To that end, *ARL* included in that issue an article on Northwestern University's electronic reserve policy. According to author Brian Nielsen, manager of the school's Learning Technologies Group, Academic Technologies, Northwestern "affirmed that uses of electronic files distributed over the network in a manner which satisfies the four factors are protected under the law as fair use."[10]

DOCUMENTING EARLY EXPERIMENTATION AND INNOVATION

In August 1996, George Soete, organizational development consultant with ARL, posted a call to the e-reserve list soliciting input for a new publication. The publication, *Transforming Libraries: Issues and Innovations In Electronic Reserves,* was to report on libraries that are providing services in creative and exciting ways and to put readers in touch with those who are leading technological change in libraries all over North America. The topic chosen for the first issue was electronic reserves. Although he was interested in technical innovations, Soete specifically solicited libraries that offered new approaches to service issues.

The inaugural issue of *Transforming Libraries* was published in October 1996, with Jeff Rosedale as editorial advisor. It posed a series of key questions for planners (including who will build the system and how will copyright be handled). It also included summaries of the then-current systems of San Diego State, Duke, and Northwestern, as well as five other university implementations. The publication looked beyond libraries and to a faculty using an electronic reserve system, the UMI electronic reserve product based on the ProQuest system, and the Copyright Clearance Center's electronic reserves permission service. Its concluding sentence again noted ARL's and the library community's interpretation of copyright for electronic reserves: "In the meantime, libraries will continue to rely on the fair-use doctrine as described in section 107 of the copyright law as the foundation for implementing electronic reserve services."[11]

ELECTRONIC RESERVE OPERATIONS IN ARL LIBRARIES

Transforming Libraries was not the only ARL publication to focus on electronic reserves. In May 1999, ARL published "Electronic Reserves Operations in ARL Libraries," SPEC Kit 245, compiled by Cindy Kristof, document delivery librarian at Kent State University. The Systems and Procedures Exchange Center (SPEC) Kit includes a flyer that summarizes the status of a current area of interest, the survey sent to ARL member libraries, documentation on the topic, and a reading list.

Of the fifty-six academic institutions that responded to the survey, thirty-two offer electronic and print-based reserves, and twenty-four offer only print-based reserve services. For the twenty-five with operational systems, most began offering their electronic reserves in 1998, with a pilot project in 1997. Most of the libraries not currently offering electronic reserves are still in the research and planning stage, and only two are not planning to offer an electronic reserve service. Ten respondents cited copyright as their primary concern; other issues were of less concern to those not offering an electronic reserve service. The survey also included questions about type and quantity of material in the system, hardware and software choices, budgetary issues, staffing, evaluation, and copyright concerns.

Most libraries in the survey have established a copyright policy for electronic reserves, and most do not pay the cost of obtaining copyright permissions for materials placed on electronic reserves. Just under half use the Copyright Clearance Center, and nearly 60 percent indicated that electronic reserves had helped to initiate campus discussions of intellectual property issues. Two libraries drafted new policy statements as a result of those conversations, one an internal policy for electronic reserves and the other a university-wide policy.

The SPEC Kit contains the University of Connecticut's draft electronic reserve policy, excerpts of the University of Georgia's guide to understanding copyright and educational fair use, and handouts from Georgia Institute of Technology. Also included are publications from

Iowa State, University of Kentucky, McMaster University, Massachusetts Institute of Technology, University of Michigan, Pennsylvania State University, Princeton University, University of Virginia, and Virginia Tech University. Evaluation forms used by Cornell and Kent State and a list of selected resources complete the publication.

KEEPING CURRENT ELECTRONICALLY: THE ARL-ERESERVE DISCUSSION LIST

The final example of ARL's commitment to electronic reserves is the establishment and maintenance of the electronic reserve discussion list, arl-ereserve forum (arl-ereserve@arl.org).[12] Established in 1993, the unmoderated list provides a forum for discussion of issues surrounding management of electronic reserves within libraries. New technologies can be the catalyst for transforming instructional support. This transformation raises technical, policy, and intellectual property questions. The list aims to encourage exploration of topics such as hardware and software selection, policy development, copyright concerns, and project reports and case studies.

CONCLUSION

The Association of Research Libraries continues to monitor new developments in electronic reserve technologies and implementations in research libraries, as well as intellectual property policy issues surrounding electronic reserves. ARL has played an active role in encouraging research libraries to implement electronic reserve systems and will continue to do so. Along with other library organizations, ARL encourages librarians in research and academic libraries to review copyright policies established by other institutions. Most important, ARL continues to believe that the U.S. copyright law protects electronic reserve services.

NOTES

1. "Electronic Reserve Rooms Bring New Business and Legal Challenges to Publishers, Librarians, and Bookstores," *PSP Bulletin* 8, no. 3 (fall 1994): 10.

2. Ibid., 11.
3. The final report is available at www.uspto.gov/web/offices/com/doc/ ipnii/index.html.
4. Mary E. Jackson, "CONFU Concludes; ARL Rejects Guidelines," *ARL; A Bimonthly Newsletter of Research Library Issues and Actions,* no. 192 (June 1997): 3.
5. Ibid., 2.
6. Report available at www.uspto.gov/web/offices/dcom/olia/confu/ concltoc.html.
7. Report available at www.uspto.gov/web/offices/dcom/olia/confu/ confurep.htm.
8. Statement available at www.arl.org/info/frn/copy/fairuse.html.
9. David Green, "CONFU Continues? Is it Time to Re-Group?" *ARL; A Bimonthly Newsletter of Research Library Issues and Actions,* no. 192 (June 1997): 5.
10. Brian Nielsen, "Northwestern Affirms Fair Use through Practice; Electronic Reserve Policy, System Developed," *ARL; A Bimonthly Newsletter of Research Library Issues and Actions,* no. 192 (June 1997): 6.
11. George Soete, "Transforming Libraries: Issues and Innovations in Electronic Reserves," SPEC Kit 217 (Washington, D.C.: Association of Research Libraries, 1996), 31.
12. Additional information on the arl-ereserve forum may be found at www. cni.org/Hforums/arl-ereserve/.

CONCLUSION

The story of the establishment, development, and growth of electronic reserve systems is important for a number of reasons. Principally, it shows how libraries can exercise leadership in joining technology and service on campuses in a unique way—one that goes beyond the traditional roles of publishers and computing professionals. Libraries and librarians are using their energy, creativity, and service mission to harness the transformational force of technology. Electronic reserves is one of the new ways they are meeting the information needs of students and scholars.

Many have speculated that electronic reserves is nothing more than a "way station" service between the print and electronic worlds. Someday, perhaps before too long, it will be possible to acquire enough material in electronic form to make in-house scanning obsolete and redundant. By and large, librarians would shed no tears if this were to prove true; few, if any, of us consider it our highest calling to reformat published materials—except, of course, for preservation and archival purposes.

In order to make the most of this information interregnum, library and information professionals must help fulfill the promise of electronic means of retrieval, storage, and use of information in direct support of instruction. Courseware, distance education, and strategic partnering of educational institutions will materially change the process of higher education. Librarians need to be poised to help, explain, and facilitate access. Doing so means continuing to acquire, store, organize, and preserve that information with a new flexibility. Librarians cannot succeed without adapting to the rapidly changing circumstances, tools, formats, and environments that now characterize teaching and learning.

We stand at the edge of a fascinating divide in higher education. On one side is the treatment of even the most generic information as a marketable commodity; schools are operated first and foremost as businesses, with unprecedented energies devoted to marketing and entrepreneurial activity; the Internet is turning itself over to e-commerce and high-bandwidth entertainment. These trends, against a legislative backdrop characterized by the passage of the Digital Millennium Copyright Act and UCITA, are cause for significant concern among libraries and librarians.

On the other side of this divide is the treatment of information and scholarship as a social good. Many recall that the profession of librarianship was founded on the basis of a commitment to community service. ARL has established SPARC in an attempt to give the power of scholarship back to the scholars and to fight back against the absurd economic leverage enjoyed by journal publishers in the sciences. The inherently democratizing force of widely available information and the power of peer-to-peer communication and sharing has been clearly demonstrated by this past year's Napster story. The Internet is serving as a fertile ground for the exchange of prepublications, conference proceedings, and interactive real-time discussions.

Somewhere, perhaps only reluctantly negotiating these opposing directions, stands the college or research library of the twenty-first century. The library will continue to serve as a place where people with different needs and interests come together as a community. Certainly it will have to reach beyond the books, desks, shelves, and walls that have characterized library service in the past. Look, then, at the story of the development of electronic reserves in the context of information evolution—for electronic reserves is definitely evolution, not revolution. Nobody, not even the most cautious publisher, needs to lose any sleep over this natural extension of the library's role on campus.

GLOSSARY

ALA Model Policy: Short for *ALA Model Policy Concerning College and University Photocopying for Classroom, Research, and Library Reserve Use* (March 1982). Although not part of copyright law, this document has long been considered a source for reserve copyright policies.

ASCII: Acronym for the American Standard Code for Information Interchange. Pronounced *ask-ee*. In the context of electronic reserves, this refers to a text-only file format.

Click-through URL: A hotlink in an online public access catalog that gives a user direct access to an electronic resource (for example, using the MARC 856 field).

CONFU Guidelines: The Conference on Fair Use issued a draft set of guidelines that sought to define fair use in the electronic reserve context. Ultimately no agreement could be reached, so the document represents a set of compromises that neither side could stand behind. Nonetheless, it remains useful as a discussion tool for issues and strategies. See Mary Jackson's and Laura Gasaway's chapters for more information on electronic reserves and copyright.

Coursepack: Typically a photocopied anthology of assigned or recommended readings, produced and assembled by a bookstore or other commercial enterprise. Coursepacks can now be made available in digital form on CD-ROM. Considered consumable items, they are usually excluded from library reserve collections.

Gopher: The immediate predecessor to browser-based, point-and-click navigation of Internet resources, gopher relied on selecting successive entries from hierarchical menus.

Homegrown system: A software package assembled from off-the-shelf or open source components.

License: Virtually all access by libraries to electronic products and services is governed by licensing agreements. Licenses can curtail or expand rights given to libraries under copyright law. Institutions interested in providing electronic reserve services should negotiate licensing agreements that include associated uses wherever possible.

NT: An acronym referring to Microsoft's Windows New Technology software, introduced in the mid-1990s as its operating system for businesses. Succeeded by Microsoft Windows 2000.

OCR (optical character recognition): A technology used to convert image files into text files, using software that "reads" page images. Note that converting images to text always requires editing to correct errors rendered by the conversion software.

ODBC: A database protocol used by many common programs, such as Microsoft Access.

Open source: Software that allows free distribution and no restriction on modifying the source code. This encourages development, extension, and experimentation. Linux is an example of an open source operating system that has enjoyed some success.

PDF: Adobe's Portable Document Format, a popular cross-platform file format that is used to disseminate many kinds of information over the Internet that were formerly available only in print. Requires Adobe's Acrobat Reader (available free) to render the page images.

Plug-in: An add-on software module to a web browser that interprets and accesses media files or other applications. Specific plug-ins may not work across all browser packages or versions.

WYSIWYG (acronym for "What you see is what you get"): Software that aims to render a page image exactly as it will be seen on a computer monitor and the printed page. Because of subtle variations in hardware and software, this is rarely universally attainable; therefore, the tongue-in-cheek WYSINQWYG has evolved, meaning, "What you see is never quite what you get."

XML: Extensible markup language, considered by many to be the next platform for web protocol development.

CONTRIBUTORS

Jeff Rosedale took a leading role in the electronic reserve community in the mid-1990s and founded the ACRL electronic reserves discussion group in 1996. He has published and lectured on this topic, and his work has received international attention. Rosedale is currently assistant library director at Manhattanville College in Purchase, New York. Previously, he studied and worked in numerous capacities at Columbia University. He maintains the Electronic Reserves Clearinghouse web site at www.mville.edu/Administration/staff/Jeff_Rosedale.

Pascal V. Calarco is currently interim head of automation services for the Virginia Commonwealth University (VCU) Libraries. He has been in the area of digital libraries since 1997 and has worked on several electronic reserve proposals and projects at Yale University and VCU since 1996. He graduated in 1995 from McGill University in Montreal, Canada, with a master's degree in library and information studies.

M. Claire Dougherty is head of digital media services at the Northwestern University Library. She held the position of reserve/multimedia services librarian at Northwestern University from 1995 to 1998 and a joint Library/IT appointment as director of the campus New Media Center from 1998 to 2000. She is a campus specialist in metadata, digital imaging, audio and video streaming, and copyright. Dougherty received her master's degree in library science from Rosary College (Dominican University) in 1995.

Jeremy Frumkin is the digital development/metadata librarian at the University of Arizona Main Library. He works with the library's digital library initiatives team to develop tools and content to support the goal of building a fully functional digital library. Frumkin is a strong advocate of open source software, with an emphasis on its use in libraries. He is the creator and maintainer of the Open Source Digital Library System project, a collaborative effort to build a freely available, next-generation digital library system.

Laura N. Gasaway has been director of the law library and professor of law at the University of North Carolina since 1985. She teaches courses in intellectual property and cyberspace law in the law school and law librarianship and legal resources in the School of Information and Library Science. She obtained a bachelor's degree and a master's degree in library science from Texas Woman's University in 1967 and 1968, respectively, and a J.D. degree from the University of Houston in 1973. Before coming to Chapel Hill, she held the same position at the University of Oklahoma from 1975 to 1984 and at the University of Houston from 1973 to 1975.

A past president of the American Association of Law Libraries and a fellow of the Special Libraries Association, Gasaway has chaired various committees of both associations, including their copyright committees. She served on the American Bar Association's Accreditation Committee from 1987 to 1995 and represented the AAUP at the fair-use conferences (for the National Information Infrastructure). She has written widely on copyright and law library management and is a frequent speaker on these issues.

Clyde W. Grotophorst is associate university librarian/library systems at George Mason University in Fairfax, Virginia. He holds a master's degree in library science from the University of Tennessee and has been active in library automation since the early 1980s. He turned to open source development projects such as OSCR after a successful stint as a shareware author (BIBL, InfoPop). He currently serves on the board of trustees for the Loudoun County Public Library.

Bud Hiller is a web access consultant in the information services and resources department at Bucknell University. He initiated a pilot program of electronic reserves in 1996 with fifteen courses. Since then, the e-reserve system has grown to more than four hundred courses with thousands of items available online. A graduate of the University of North Carolina-Chapel Hill, Hiller earned his master's degree in education at Georgia State University.

Mary E. Jackson is the senior program officer for access services for the Association of Research Libraries (ARL) in Washington, D.C. She directs the North American Interlibrary Loan and Document Delivery (NAILDD) project and chairs its protocol implementors group. Jackson is an internationally recognized authority on interlibrary loan, document delivery, resource sharing, and copyright issues. Her major publications include "Measuring the Performance of Interlibrary Loan Operations in North American Research and College Libraries," "Uses of Document Delivery Services," and "Maximizing Access, Minimizing Cost." Before her affiliation with ARL, she managed the interlibrary loan department at the University of Pennsylvania. She holds a bachelor's degree from Carroll College and a master's degree in library science from Drexel University.

Philip R. Kesten is a vice president and co-founder of Docutek Information Systems as well as an associate professor of physics and chairman of the physics department at Santa Clara University in Santa Clara, California. He holds a bachelor's degree in physics from the Massachusetts Institute of Technology and a Ph.D. in high-energy particle physics from the University of Michigan. Kesten has been designing and implementing large-scale software systems for more than twenty-five years, including Card File, a research data system used in the mid-1970s at Syracuse University, and CDFDB, the database system for the Collider Detector particle physics experiment at Fermilab.

Wayne R. Perryman is chair of the access services department and acquisitions librarian at Humboldt State University Library. Before joining the Humboldt State library faculty in 1995, he was deputy assistant director for technical services and chair of the acquisitions and serials department in the General Libraries of the University of Texas at Austin, where he worked for fourteen years. He also held positions in the Stanford University Libraries and the Santa Clara County Free Library System. In all, Perryman has had more than thirty-five years of library experience.

Steven J. Schmidt is the access services team leader at the IUPUI (Indiana University-Purdue University Indianapolis) University Library and project director for ERROL, that institution's award-winning electronic reserve project. In addition to his work with electronic reserves and library automation, Schmidt serves as a part-time adjunct professor for the IU School of Library and Information Science and is a frequent speaker at conferences and workshops.

Lorre Smith is librarian for Digital Library Initiatives for the University Libraries, University at Albany, State University of New York, where she led the implementation of electronic reserves in 1998. She has conducted systematic studies of electronic reserves systems specifications and electronic reserves policies in U.S. libraries and has spoken on general electronic reserves policies and electronic reserves policies regarding copyright restrictions and fair use. Smith earned a master's degree in library science in 1978 from Indiana University.

INDEX

Index